Referrals And...

Recommendations,
Introductions,
Endorsements,
Testimonials,
Reviews,
And
Word of Mouth

Dean Willeford
With JoJo Dean Illustrations

First Printing, 2014

Printed in the United States of America

ISBN-13: 978-1497365544
ISBN-10: 1497365546
BISAC: Business   &   Economics/   Sales   &   Selling   /   Management

Referrals And...

Recommendations,
Introductions,
Endorsements,
Testimonials,
Reviews,
And
Word of Mouth

A Guide to Explosive Business Growth

Table of Content

About the Author

 Dean Willeford is an Authority Marketing expert, author and speaker whose focus is to show sales professional, small business owners, entrepreneurs, and professionals how to get more customers, sell more products/services , build a powerful brand and establish themselves as an authority leader in their fields.

He uses referrals, "expert" publications and networking techniques to make you the "Go To" person in your field.

Dean has more than 30 years of marketing, financial and sales experience. He served as CEO of United Publishers, a major yellow pages company, where brought sale from less than $1 millions to over $8 million in less than three years. He has sales experience as a stock broker, mortgage loan broker and IRS Registered Tax Preparer. He is an avid free enterprise activist and after leaving the corporate world, he founded and built BDS Consulting Group by helping hundreds of small businesses to start, grow and prosper for the last 26 years.

He graduated from University of Southern California (USC) and did graduate work at Califonia State University. At USC he was an All America swimmer, and later a member of the Olympic team in waterpolo, and member of the Waterpolo and Swimming Hall of Fame. Currently President of the Nevada Olympians and is working to bring the Winter Olympics to the Reno-Tahoe area.

Dean is the author of four business books, including Referrals And... ,which all can be found on Amazon.com and other outlets. You can see his LinkedIn Profile at www.linkedin.com/in/deangotoexpert/.

If you are serious about growing your business or profession contact Dean at BDSConsult@gmail.com or call 775-827-1775.

About the Illustrator

JoJo Dean has been working with self published authors with the idea of  providing a different "bend" on traditional business books, and a little bit of humor to what some people may think is a "dry" subject.

She hopes her illustrations capture your interest as well as the content does. She loves to create characters that explain the value of the author's ideas. She aims with every book to engage and invite the reader to gain valuable information with a smile on your face and a desire to read on.

You can contact her at BDSConsult@gmail.com.

Thanks for buying our book.

Please review this book on Amazon.com .

We need your feedback to make the next version better. We want to hear from you. As the reader of this book, you are our most important commentators. We value your feedback.

You can email or write us about what you did or didn't like about the book. We would like to know what areas you would like to see us publish.

When you contact us, please be sure to include the book's title as well as your name and e-mail address.

Email: BDSConsult@gmail.com
Mail: Xpert Publisher
        Attn: Reader Feedback
        3680 Grant Drive, Suite N
        Reno, Nevada, 89509

Introductions

Most people think of a referral as something similar to the dictionary definition - "to direct a person to someone for information or anything else required". I like to think it has a much broader definition for purposes of conducting business. It includes the concepts of endorsement, recommendation, testimonial, positive review, "word-of-mouth" and even an introduction. Each has a slightly different shade of meaning. However, all suggest a positive view of a person, product or service.

Referrals can cover a very large spectrum; from a close personal intimate relationship between an accountant and his client, or a doctor with his patient. Or, it can be as simple as a recommendation of a car dealer suggesting a customer go to have a trailer hitch installed by a local automobile accessory shop. The spectrum has different sales cycles and different time periods to cultivate a relationship with those who can send business your way.

This book suggests hundreds of ways to generate referrals, but you should only use those that fit your particular type of business, practice, or sales circumstances. All are governed by some simple basic principles which are, common to every customer/supplier relationship.

There are really only five simple steps to creating a referral dominated business or profession.

1. Establish a mindset that you have something valuable to offer.
2. Exceed expectations on the delivery of your service/product promise.
3. Find a few referral strategies that you find most comfortable and that are practical for your business. Integrate those strategies into a system you use *daily*.
4. Ask for and expect referrals, recommendation, introduction, endorsements, testimonials, reviews and positive word-of-mouth.
5. Continue to demonstrate gratitude, appreciation and thanks for every person or organization that helps you.

Every customer/client/patient has a problem to solve, or a need to satisfy. It's your job to spread the word through a network of satisfied customers, clients or patients. Prove you are the best possible choice. The more people you have recommending you, the easier, more profitable, cost-effective, productive and satisfying your job becomes.

Marketing by referral is by far is the best way to build your business, practice and sales. Business by referral has the best return on investment (ROI). Referral business tends to buy more, buy more frequently, refund less, and cost less to attract. There is usually less stress involved in the selling and purchase process. The closing rate is usually more than 90%. Referral sources tend to become tireless, silent sales forces that cheer lead for you. Your referral network becomes self-sustaining with just a modicum of effort.

Most businesses use the "prayer "method for getting referrals. They do nothing to stimulate referrals and pray people will send them business. Although it is a method, it does not work well. It is slow and inefficient. Instead you must explicitly ask for referrals and recommendations. The pray method works a lot better when you implement the suggestions in the book.

How well does referral marketing work? Let me show you a real case study from one of my own businesses. I'm only going to show you four referral sources, but there are many more. Almost every client has referred at least one other business. It shows how four sources referred 19 other businesses. Only one of the nineteen did not become a client, for a closing rate of 94%. This a typical closing ratio for referral business.

1.   Surfboard manufacturer referred:
                      a skateboard manufacturer.
                      a cabinet manufacturer.
                          which led to a photographer,
                              which led to a clothing manufacturer.
                      a general contractor
                          which led to an audio engineer.
                          which led to a pet grooming business.
                          which led to an automobile restoration business,

which led to a interior decorator.

2.   A restaurant referred:
another restaurant,
    which led to another restaurant.

3.   A photographer referred:
another photographer,
    which led to another photographer,
    which lead to another photographer,
    which lead to a caterer,
    which lead to a disc jockey .

4.   An automobile repair business referred:
another automobile repair business.
a retail tire business,
    which led to a chiropractor.

When you are referred, it implies an obligation to provide quality products and/or services. That's true, but it also brings with it a responsibility that you perform to a higher level of expectations. When referred, you should take it is as great compliment. They have confidence that you will validate their judgment of you. Everyone that is asked to refer worries about their own reputation. Will the person being referred live up to their expectation? Take that responsibility, perform brilliantly and your referral network will expand rapidly.

There are only 29 or so *basic* strategies, but there are as many twists to each strategy as there are kinds of businesses. This book is filled with stories and examples of how the basic strategies are utilized. They are meant to inspire you to create your own variation and show you it has already been done successfully.

There really is nothing new in referral marketing, but it may be new to you. Some stories and examples may apply to you directly, but most can be adapted to your particular situation. They will open your mind and suggest you apply your unique talents, personality and ingenuity to a strategy.

This book is organized into five parts:

1)	Part One gives you the basic foundations to all referral strategies. You must execute these things to make referral marketing work well.

2)	Part Two talks about how to clarify and define your business and brand so referral sources can have something to hang their hat on. It shows you how to communicate your message to your customers and your referral network.

3)	Part Three gives you a list of 15 sources that you can look to for referrals.

4)	Part Four shows you how to organize and follow up on the recommendations you get.

5)	Part Five has 29 techniques and many examples of how to use them in real-life. Each one of the strategies has hundreds of variations depending on your business and personal characteristics.

Your Guide

There is one other introduction I would like to make. His name is Hank.

 He is here on the left, and has agreed to help me introduce the techniques, strategies, and methods in the book. I know him well because he is one of my clients. He is well-qualified because he developed his business by word-of-mouth, referrals, and recommendations. Almost all of his business came to him in this way.

He used to sell real estate in Southern California, but he was not happy with that, so he moved to the great Pacific Northwest and started a fishing gear business. Fishing was his first love and real passion. He liked the outdoor life and the freedom of being self-employed. His new daily "business suit" is now a baseball cap and fishing togs. Not only is he a salesman for his company and products, traveling the Northwest, but he ships his products all over the United States, and he does well.

If you follow Hank's and my advice, I think you will do surprisingly well also.

We feel strongly that referral marketing is the single most effective marketing strategy for any business. We use lots of shoulds, musts, have tos and imperative statements to encourage you to make a big commitment to this form of marketing. It's not necessarily easy, but it is a lot easier, cheaper and more rewarding than any other sales and marketing method.

I wrote this book because hardly anyone I have dealt with over the years *asked* for referrals, recommendations, testimonials or reviews. Yet, I built two businesses from the ground up almost exclusively by referral. I give out referrals constantly, but I'm virtually never asked for one. This says to me that there is a giant educational hole to be filled. My mission is to show the reader how to ask for and use referrals to expand their business and influence.

Use of terms

We use the term business to means a trade, a practice, profession, and also nonprofit entities. The terms customers, clients, and patients are used interchangeably. Those terms are synonymous in the sense that they include anyone who gives you money for your products or services. Entities may be referred to as companies, corporations, Limited Liability Company (LLC), partnerships, and individuals for the purpose of referrals. Networking is meeting people and cultivating mutually beneficial, give and take, win-win relationships that *support each other*.

Action workbook

You must take action to get big rewards. From experience I have found only two percent of the people who buy this book will take the action steps to jump forward.

Pick two to five of the strategies in the book that fit your business and answer the questions at the end of each section. Look for the recommended action steps designated by a check mark (√). It also lets you look back to see other steps you can take on your journey to referral success. The very act of writing down your actions will help you accomplish them. This will put you on the road to action, explosive growth and a referral dominated business.

We are a "hands on"organization, and want to see you succeed. After you the follow the strategies for 30 days, give us a call or e mail with your success story and or questions. BDSConsult@gmail.com or 775-827-1775. Those success stories will be included in future editions of this book.

Part 1

Foundation

Foundation

Doing business by referral is the natural way to do business. It springs from the five basic concepts described below. People will naturally want to do business with you because the system described in this book will make you the natural choice in your line of work. The system cultivates the natural tendency to do business with, and refer, people you **know and trust**. All other things being equal (and sometimes unequal), people do business with a friend.

If you truly believed you have something valuable for your customers, clients, patients you have not only the right to ask for referrals, but also an obligation, because the value you provide cannot be duplicated by most other vendors.

1.1   ASK

"And I say unto you ask, and it shall be given to you; seek, and you shall find, knock, and it shall be opened unto you." Luke 11:9

What great marketing advice. This is the essence of marketing yourself or a business. Seek out the market that you want, knock on many doors, in many ways, and ask for the order.

The basis of all referrals is your mind set. You must believe you have something valuable to offer. You must believe you are doing a real service that people want and need. There is an ocean of referral business available. You can go down to the ocean with a teaspoon or a bucket – it all up to you as to the number of referrals you want. The supply is unlimited. However, you must *ask* for them continually.

Once you have a positive mindset about referrals, the MOST important thing you can do to get referrals is to ASK. People will not be afraid to refer to you if you are already doing a great job. There are hundreds of ways to ask which we will cover in Part 5. You can ask aggressively, because there are many ways to ask without offending people. Successful people are not easily discouraged from asking for referrals and recommendations. Timidity will get you nowhere.

Ask is an active, not passive word. You must ask for referral from those people with whom you have developed a positive beneficial relationship. Doing a good job is not enough to insure you have a continuing stream of productive referrals.

Sounds simple enough, but it is amazing the percentage of people who never ask for referrals. I have had dozens of people work on and in my home and many rental properties, yet I've never had a single one ask for a referral. I have never had a vendor ask for a referral or introduction to any of the dozens of other businesses in my office complex or business portfolio.

Why you don't ask.

1. **Fear of rejection**. Everyone fears rejection. It makes you feel small and unworthy if someone rejects you. That same fear is why salespeople do not ask a prospective customer to buy. It is a well know fact that most salespeople never ask for the order. Fear is the reason most people dislike public

speaking, asking for a date or making changes. It is a powerful emotion that stops many actions and limits performance. The fear originates from a lack of confidence. If your mindset and attitude is that you do a great job and are expert at your profession, fear will be overwhelmed by your confidence.

2. **You don't want to appear to be "needy" or struggling to get business**. Make it clear your reason for asking for referrals is your desire to expand your business and service your customers better. Most all businesses are trying to grow and people know it. Make your central theme growth and prosperity.

3. **You are afraid you have not earned referrals**. If you don't feel you have done an excellent job, you will naturally hesitate to ask for more. Do the best job you can and you will have a different attitude. Since you have done your best above all others you will know, you will earn the right to ask for more.

 *Write down why you don't ask*_____
_____

Why customers don't refer.

1. **They don't want to push a salesperson on to a friend or customer.** The reason people are reluctant to refer you is that you have not done a good job assuring the customer you will not "high pressure" or create any ill will. Remind the customer how they became your customer and how many benefits they have derived from your relationship. After all, wouldn't their referral also benefit from your product or service?

2. **People don't know exactly what you do or products you have.** It is quite common that your current customers know you principally by what you do for them, but are unaware of other services or products you have.

A car repair customer may know you repair brakes, but didn't know you also do alignment services. Your customer might know you have a great restaurant, but were unaware you also do catering. Be sure your clients know of all the products and service you provide

3. **People don't know how they might benefit from a referral**. This reason is closely aligned with the products and service you provide. There are many hidden or unexpected benefits that your service provides, but customers don't know. You need to remind them.

4. **Fear they might upset an existing relationship**.
If you are doing a great job for your current customers, they will not fear passing on the benefits you provide. So the solution is to assure your customer you will be professional, competent and handle their referral with "Kid gloves". Tell the referral source *exactly* how you will contact the referral and what you will do. You will provide all the benefits you gave the referral source.

5. **They can't think of anyone who might benefit from your services.**
Everyone knows other people, customers, acquaintances whom they can refer. Your job is to remind them of those specific people you would be interest in talking with. An insurance agent might say "do you know anyone who would needs life insurance?", instead, how about, " Have any of your friends just gotten married or just has a baby?"

Many times people need a "hook" that is more specific to jog their memories. A CPA who is known for preparing corporate taxes needs to remind his clients he also does individual tax returns, thereby opening up the possibility of doing company employee and stockholder's taxes.

 List each person you will ask for a referral in the next 30 days.

_____

_____

_____

1.2 Do a Great Job.

A major pillar of creating a referral dominated business is to deliver on what you say you will do. The better you are at providing what your customers, clients, and patients want, the more referrals you will get. You must:

- Always deliver what you promise.
- Exceed the customer's expectations.
- Get it done on time.
- Get it right the first time.

Deliver

This sounds so simple, but it is ignored by most businesses because they are not customer centered. This cannot be overly emphasized. You MUST do what you say you will do. This is the way you build trust with the customer. The trust is what will get you referrals. If they can trust you to deliver, in their minds, they can trust you with the people they know.

It is so easy to build trust. You can do it in so many ways, and it usually takes so little to do it. If you say you will be at a meeting at 4:00 o'clock, be there at 4:00 o'clock. If you say you will complete the job on a certain date, be sure you do. Be sure the product/service is no less than you promised. If you tell the customer the product or project will meet certain standards, be sure it does. Give guarantees and stand behind them. You want to have such good service that when people talk about you, they say such things as "You can count on him.", or "She always delivers."

Of course, there are circumstances that are occasionally beyond your control. If you can't fix it, let the customer know ASAP. Explain the circumstances, and offer solutions, apologies and reparations. By purchasing from you, the customer has agreed to your original promise and expects it to be delivered. Most people are reasonable, and will accept your fix. More importantly, it shows you care, are flexible, and are trying to provide a solution.

Once you get a reputation, either good or bad, it will stick to you. The reason bad reviews on Web sites and on the internet are so deadly, is because you don't have a chance to correct the problem before they are disseminated to the world.

Little things are so important, but are powerful reputation builders.
- Return phone calls quickly. Customers and prospects hate to be kept hanging without answers.
- Deliver ahead of promised dates.
- Add unexpected bonuses, if possible.
- Send thank you cards or messages.
- You need to step into the shoes of the customer and anticipate what they want.
- Apologize and fix it quickly when you make a mistake.

Exceed Expectations

Not only deliver, exceed expectations. You need to step into the shoes of the customer and anticipate what they want. I was looking for something in a "big box" home improvement store and stopped one of their "associates" to ask where it was. This has happened before, so I expected the associate to tell me it was on isle X, but the young man said " It is on isle 15" *and* escorted me to the isle and section where it was. He then asked if he could help further. As it turned out, I did have another question. If he had not escorted me, I would have been the same situation I started with, still needing help. As a result, I tend to go to that store over a similar one that is only a block away.

In Michael LeBoeuf's great little book, <u>How to Win Customers and Keep them for Life</u>, he tells a story about a custom in Southern Louisiana called "lagniappe" (pronounced lan-yap).It means "something extra". If a customer asked for five pounds of sugar, the shop owner would carefully measure out five pounds on the scale, then he would add a little free to the order and say "lagniappe". This was the shopkeeper's way of saying I'm giving you what you want plus a little extra for being a loyal customer. The lesson here, of course, is reward the buyer by delivering more than you promised or they expected.

Whether you are a business or a sale representative, your rewards for good customer service are:
1. Increased market share.
2. The repeat business leads to larger and more frequent sales.
3. More customers.
4. Fewer complaints and less time solving problems.
5. Less marketing, advertising and promotional expenses.
6. A great personal and company reputation.

Stand out from your competitors

Great service sets you apart from competitors. Since there is usually little difference in product and service offerings between companies, you tend to stand out because of great service.

Not only does great service make your customers feel better, it also makes you feel better. When you give great service your energy and feeling about your job are also enhanced. Who doesn't feel better about themselves after delivering great products and services? You get more unsolicited referrals and it makes asking for them much easier.

1.3 Giving

People prefer to work with givers, not takers.

As the famous public speaker and sales master, Zig Ziglar, reminds us, "the more we help people get what they want, the more you get what you want." The founder of Forbes business magazine, B.C. Forbes, said, "when businesses realize that they serve themselves best, when they serve others the most".

You should strive to create a partnership of *mutual* benefits with your customers, clients, patients. You need to establish rapport, commonality of interest, cooperation, and work toward helping the customer get what they want. When you have a commonality of interest, it allows you to anticipate problems, challenges, and opportunities. Referrals are all about giving. Give the best service to your customers.

Go the extra mile to solve problems, find solutions. Since so few businesses extend themselves, your extras become notable and unique to your business. In most cases the extra service will not even cost anything. Try it create a partnership to solve the customer's problem. The partnership allows you to influence the buyer. Work to become absolutely dependable and offer an exchange of benefits.

Respect your customers. Do *for* them, not *to* them. You are trying to confirm the relationship and create a win- win relationship. You are trying to *open* the sale not *close* the sale. Closing the sale will happen naturally if you have your customer's best interests at heart. Closing the sale implies an end of the relationship. You should be trying to open the relationship for now and the future. Work to become absolutely dependable and offer an exchange of benefits.

Your best future customer is your current customer. Think of the life time value of your customer. Look at the life time value as an annuity where your good work creates residual value. They will give you many times the benefits of a single sale. For example, if you repair someone's automobile correctly, with genuine care, they will come back to you for a lifetime of service. The service becomes not a one-time $70 sale, but years of $70 sales. You cannot run a successful business, or be a successful salesperson unless people come back to you over and over again. A restaurant is a perfect example of a business that could not survive without returning customers. Work to become unquestioningly reliable. Do what you say, and then some.

Not only will a good customer come back to purchase your product and service again and again, they will send many referrals and new customers to you. When you create the atmosphere of trust, quality of service and product, customers will be willing to send their friends, acquaintances etc. to you unsolicited, but will also give you referrals when you ask.

Be a "connector". One of the best things you can give is a referral to other problem solvers. Try to connect and introduce people to one another. When you learn of a need a customer has that you can't solve, try to connect them to someone in your network who can. Speak enthusiastically of your referral. Offer to make a personal introduction if needed.

Jay Abraham, a legend in the marketing business, makes these six golden rules of giving:
> "You cannot service too much.
> You cannot educate too much.
> You cannot inform too much.
> You cannot offer too much follow-up and
>   follow through too far.
> You cannot make ordering too easy.

You cannot make calling or coming into your place of business too easy."

When you do something for a client, don't ask or expect immediate repayment. Be genuine and giving. Don't create resentment or an obligation by asking something in return. You don't want to create the feeling that they owe you. When you do enough good, I can assure you it will return to you many times over.

Be responsive.

Your clients and customers expect you to respond to them. Return telephone calls and e-mail messages quickly. Customers /clients hate to be left twisting in the wind. Even if you don't have the answer, let the customer know that they are on your mind and you will respond fully when you have the answer. Attorneys and other professionals who tend to get their payments up front are the worst offenders. Customers tend to think "well they have my money and they don't care anymore". Unfortunately many professionals abuse this trust. If you want a good reputation with your clients, get back to them. This is one of the easiest things to do, yet it is most destructive to your reputation when you don't do it.

Not being service oriented leads to loss of reputation and loss of customers. Unfortunately, customers won't tell you your service is poor, but they will tell others. According to a US News and World Report magazine report, they found 68% of customers are lost because of poor service and poor compliant resolution. Even worse, out of 25 dissatisfied customers:

- One customer complains
- 24 are dissatisfied but don't complain

- 24 of the non-complainers tell between 10-20 other people about the bad experience.

These non-complainers silently undermine your business and make it more difficult to get new customers. *And, you never know about it.*

Don'ts

Don't drop a lot of marketing or promotion material on a referral source. If they ask for information about your business, then, by all means send data, but don't over load them.

Don't criticize your competitors. Others may wonder what you are saying about them behind their backs.

Don't ask for referrals or favors immediately after you have done a good deed if it appears that the request is a quid pro quo.

1.5 Law of Reciprocity.

Not only is it necessary to do an outstanding job and provide extraordinary service, but there is an undeniable, hidden, human social Law of Reciprocity that is at work in generating referral. Referrals take advantage of this universal law. Just like a tide lifts all boats, the Law of Reciprocity lubricates all transactions between people.

What is the Law of Reciprocity? The dictionary says, it means to give or feel in return. Accord to the brilliant book <u>Influence</u>, by Dr. Robert B. Cialdini, this is a rule of social interaction that says we should try to repay, in kind, what another person has provided to us. We are obligated to the future repayment of favors, gifts, invitations.

You can see the power of reciprocity in the political arena where there is a continuous exchange of favors. The very act of contributing to politicians obligates them to more strongly consider the contributor's views and requests.

The rate of donations almost doubles when direct mail fund raiser includes a small unsolicited gift like pre-address labels. The feeling of obligation, even from a stranger, drives the extra donations.

This Law is very powerful and underlies all your efforts to give and to help others. We all know the social consequences of appearing to not reciprocate. There is a general dislike for those who take, but do not attempt to return a favor.

We are not trying to perniciously obligate others, but the social custom will suggest they return the help. It becomes more powerful when we give freely without the intent of expecting a return. People don't like to be in debt to others. Let the Law of Reciprocity work its subtle magic.

1.5 Your System

You should set up a system specifically for the needs of your particular business for managing referrals. A system allows you to consistently reproduce, manage, and gives you a high return on the time and money you investment in getting referrals. A system will

obviate the need to "reinvent the wheel" each time you get referrals.

There are two parts to a system. The first part is how you will produce and ask for referrals. Since every business differs in products, services, size, employees, etc, it offers every business unique opportunities.

Part Five will show you dozens of strategies and hundreds of businesses that have adapted the basic referral methods to their businesses. You will be able to directly copy some strategies, and others you can apply a unique twist to your business. You can even use and adapted referral systems from industries entirely difference from yours. There are almost an unlimited number of models.

Your system should include specific language and verbiage to ask for referrals.

The second part of a system will include ways to follow up, manage, control and schedule referral leads you get. We will suggest an automated follow up system that can re-engage your referral consistently.

Your system should incorporate the fact that most products and services have a natural repurchase cycle. Anniversaries come around every 356 days, computer replacement averages every 36-40 months, automobiles start to look older every 3-4 years, and tax preparation happen every 12 months. Follow ups and referral requests should be scheduled more frequently around the natural sales cycle.

1.6 Commitment

To succeed with anything, including referral marketing, you must make a commitment or pledge to take the steps to make it happen.

Commit to the idea of referral marketing. Keep in mind the benefits of higher closing ratios, more efficient use of your time, higher profitability, more referrals, recommendations and positive testimonials from current customers, more loyalty and more tolerant customers. It is a lot easier than cold calling and less expensive than advertising.

Commit to set up a system to acquire and follow up new referrals and current customers. Pledge to work your system daily and methodically. Set deadlines and daily contact goal. Commit to a goal of the number of people you will bring into a referral network. Starting with only 200 you already know and adding less than 3 per day will bring over 1000 people per year to do business with, to refer to, support you and get referrals from.

Commit to learning the language and scripts for asking for referrals.

Commit to becoming an expert in your field. Write a book or articles to prove it. With e books and the internet it is easy to get "expert" status. Experts are always sought out and referred.

Commit to not give up. Preserve

Finally, commit to the finest customer service. Great customer service creates a sales force composed of your satisfied clients.

 Write down your starting commitment date_____

PART 2

Define Your Business

USP, Niche and Expertise all complement each other. Once you decide on and establish a niche, you can create a USP to make that target market want to come to you. People want to refer you. When you establish your expertise in that niche the deals are easy to close.

Define Your Business

People want to refer to people who can give them what they want, solve a problem or fulfill a desire. You must position yourself in people's minds that you are the only logical choice to fulfill their need. Why do people buy? There are two related parts to their decision.

They buy you, your products and service because it is a solution to a problem or need. People don't buy clothes; they buy style, appearance and attractiveness. People don't buy insurance; they buy security and peace of mind. So, sell to their solution and need.

Why do people refer? You solved their problem, and they liked and trusted you. The way you get people to like you is to provide great service. Great service can take many forms, courtesy, caring, attentiveness; follow up, attention to details, flexibility, anticipating their needs, etc. If someone goes into a furniture store and finds exactly what they need, but the the sales person is not pleasant, they may buy the furniture, but they won't recommend the sales person.

2.1 Your Niche

The most successful businesses are specialized and focused on a niche in their general field. People would rather deal with an expert than a generalist.

 Niche professionals have products and services that fill a particular market need better. A focused niche will help you generate more referrals. You have a stronger position *against* your competitors and *with* your clients. It gives you an unfair advantage where you know more and have better tools to perform for your customers.

For example, an employment agency will do better if they service a particular part of the employment placement market. An engineering firm is more likely to hire an employment agency that specializes in placing engineers than one that is a generalists. That's why certain employment agencies even have a specific name for the job filling services. They are called, executive recruiters, because they specialize in certain kinds of personnel and want to distinguish their niche.

If you are in real estate sales, concentrate on just a small part of the wide real estate market. Concentrate your sales effort on industrial property, or just restaurant property or a specific geographic area. If you are looking for a building in Manhattan, you will probably use an agent who only deals there.

Doctors almost always refer to a specialist. Patients have come to expect a specialist because they know they will get better, more informed care.

Your specialization separates you from the crowd, and gives your prospective clients much more confidence that you know that field better and therefore, can do a better job.

So whether you are a pet lover or a doctor, focus. You will do much better as an expert in that niche.

An Expert's Niche

People in a particular niche tend to know each other. It makes word-of-mouth and referral marketing much easier. Specializing makes it easier to attract clients. They will be drawn to your expertise and knowledge in that particular segment. You will be able to focus your marketing resources of time and money towards that market that is looking for your services.

41

Most inexperienced sales and business people fear that concentration will narrow their market and therefore they will have fewer opportunities. In fact, the opposite is true. Just be sure your niche is big enough to have plenty of little potential customers.

How do you select a niche? Ask yourself:
- What are your passionate interests?
- What are you particularly good at?
- What experiences do you have in that niche?
- Who do you know in the niche?
- What niche needs filling, or is underserviced, or new?
- What unique angle or perspective can you bring to that niche?
- What geographic area do you want to serve?
- Can your niche be broken down within specific industries, like medicine, construction, law, recreational, banking or insurance, etc.?
- Do you want to serve a particular age group, marital status, lifestyle, or sex?
- What size of company do you want to sell to? 1 to 10 employees or Fortune 500 companies?

These questions help you find your true interests and the needs of the customers. More importantly, it tells you how to use your resources. If you become a specialist in that niche, you will become known much more quickly, and referrals will come more quickly, because your market universe is much smaller. Your reputation is everything within a niche.

 ***What is your niche or specialty?*_____**

What you do.

It is important to be clear about what your business or profession is, so people can recommend you for that activity. Telling people you are a bookkeeper, a therapist, or a photographer, for example, does not tell the whole story. A bookkeeper does check reconciliation, general ledger posting; may prepare payroll and quarterly tax returns, make budget projections or business plans.. People may know you post transactions, but do not know you can prepare payroll or business plans. These are specific things people can hook on to.

Your self-imposed description that you are a photographer does not describe your real profession. They don't know that you specialize in interior photography. You work with magazines, design studios and furniture manufacturer, and have contacts in those industries. You have specialized know-how of interior lighting, angles, non distortion techniques, etc.

I can think of several incidences over the years where I found out one of my customers went elsewhere for a service I provided, because they were unaware I did it. It was my fault I didn't inform the customer of my range of services.
Make sure your supports, referral sources, and business associates know specifically what you do.

Flash Introduction

It's always handy to have a quick explanation of what you do. It should be a short, positive benefit filled statement. It is widely known as an "elevator pitch". I prefer calling it a "Flash Introduction". Not only are the answers more interesting, but they will invite more questions about you.

43

- Instead of saying, "I own a vitamin store", how about, "I counsel people on healthy nutrition and supplements at our store on Main Street". Or,
- Instead of "I'm a CPA", how about "My accounting firm helps people and businesses save taxes, and give businesses accurate numbers to help them make better business decisions". Or,
- If a dentist, tell people, " I give people great smiles at my dental office"
- In our case, we're not just publishers, "We help professionals write their "expert" book that establishes their expert status. It becomes their ultimate business card and positions them as the "go to" person in their industry."
- Insurance: "We protect you, and insure you can sleep at night"
- General Contractor: "We build moats and castles"

In other words tell people about the benefits you offer, not what you are. Try this formula from Greig Wells to create a Flash Introduction:
- "You know how (company or professionals) are looking for (insert problem)?
  I solved this
  I do this by (unique benefit statement) by (unique benefit attributed to you)."
  Example: "You know how auhors are seeking to get exposure for their books?"
  "I solved that."
  "I do this by utilizing a special Insider website and press release format that guarantees exposure on mass media like ABC, NBC Fox and NBC and social media."

 Write down your Flash Introduction

_____

_____

Once you establish a niche, you want to position yourself as an expert in that niche.

2.2 Expertise

If you are not already an expert in your business, become the "go to" authority in your field. How do you do that? Read, study, attend industry events and take continuing education classes or courses.

Surround yourself with the trappings of authority and expertise. Acquire credentials and certifications. Display those credentials in office setting. Announce those accreditations in articles, biographies, sales and promotional materials, web sites, and social media.

Titles are important to bestow expert status and authority, for example:
- President, Director, Vice President.
- Doctor, MD or PhD.

- Specialty doctors, Cardiologist, Nephrologists, Psychiatrist, Urologist, etc.
- Professor, College level expertise.
- CPA, certified by the state that you have accounting knowledge.
- Government certified specialist, Enrolled Agent (EA) certified to practice before the IRS, Actuary, and Registered Tax Preparer.
- Professional Board certifications like Orthopedic or Cosmetic surgeons.
- Judge, legal expertise
- Author implies special knowledge about a specific subject.
- CRS, Certified Residential specialists in real estate.
- CCIM, Certified Commercial Investment Member for real estate.
- MFT, certified Marriage, Family Therapist.
- Pharmacist, expert knowledge of drugs and their effects.
- Almost every professional organization has some specialized certification.

Demonstrate your authority and success by dressing well. There have been repeated studies of how much better you are received in a well-tailored business suit. Dress appropriate to your industry. Authority and status is communicated by expensive jewelry, watches and automobiles.

Perform your craft using the best tools and state of the art practices. Be up to date on new developments and trends in the business. Associate yourself with the newest products and ideas. Write articles for industry web sites, journals and newsletters. Create your own newsletter for distribution to prospects, referral sources, customers and contacts.

You can enhance your authority and expertise by authoring a book about some aspect of your business or profession. In this new electronic publishing age you have the ability to quickly and easily publish electronic books, paperback books, and even hardcover books in 60 to 90 days. A book demonstrates your expertise, your credibility and makes you a recognized authority in your field. You stand above the crowd when you can say you are a published. A book, with your name on the front cover, becomes your ultimate business card. You become a "go to" person in your business. There is less than one in a thousand that author a book on their profession.

There are many benefits to being a published author other than those above:

A published book can be the jumping off point to other related products, such as audio CDs, seminars, paid public speaking, and consulting. You can charge higher fees as almost all specialists do. You can also earn royalties of 10% to 30% of the book's selling price.

Your expert status totally changes your position. You no longer have to "pitch" the prospect; they ask you for your opinions and expert advice. For example, seldom will a person quibble with a pharmacist, judge or CPA about their field of expertise. You have the power to determine price, terms, payments, and the sales process. A new client interview centers on solutions to their needs and your product or services, not the price. All other things being equal, most of the time a prospect will go with you, a recognized published expert in your field. You increase your confidence. Use your book as your new business card in mailings, leave it behind at a sales call or a referral interview.

The author of this book offers a program called Expert Book Coach under its Xpert Publisher brand that is aimed at helping you create your book of expertise in 60 to 90 days. You can contact Dean at XpertPub@mail.com. to get your expert book created.

√ *What is your expertise?*_____

_____

_____

_____

√ *What three things do you do, or want to do, to demonstrate your expertise?*

_____

_____

_____

_____

2.3 Unique Selling Proposition (USP)

What is a Unique Selling Proposition? The USP solves a customer's problem and fulfills their desires. Why is it important that the USP is unique? It sets you apart from the competition and gives customers a reason to choose you. It is a simple concise statement that makes you stand above the competition.

Establish a Unique Selling Proposition (USP). In the 1950's Rosser Reeves, then the chairman of Ted Bates Advertising said this is the essence of your business. Your USP zeros in on what you do best. It tells your market *exactly* what service you provide and defines your strengths.

So, it is imperative you have a Unique Selling Proposition (USP) that solves their problem, gives the market what they want, AND describes your benefits. When you work for a company, the USP becomes your mission. When you work for yourself it becomes your business essence.

There are many ways to characterize the USP.
- It is the idea that sets you part from every other competitor in your industry,
- The USP should make your customers say to themselves," I would have to be crazy to do business with anyone else".
- It leads people to think that you are the only logical choice.
- The USP creates the most value in your customer's mind.
- Your USP is the singular, unique benefit that your customers can expect to receive when they buy from you instead of your competitors.

48

How do people get to know your USP? Put it on your stationery, packaging, advertising, business cards, web site, and emails. Emphasize it in your sales presentations.

Of course, you must deliver on the USP's promise.

If you say a package will be delivered "absolutely, positively overnight", it must be. When you say you have the "Ultimate Driving Machine" it needs to be a great automobile. When you claim the "lowest prices", like Wal-Mart, they need to be. If you fail to deliver on your USP it will destroy your reputation and business.

Regardless of what your USP is, you need something to hang your hat on that makes you special, notable and desirable.

Most companies have no USP. They are "me too" businesses. They *all* say "best prices and best service", so customers have no reason to use your business over any other in the category. Thumb through the yellow pages. You will see what I mean. They muddle their message by trying to be all things to all people. The reason price becomes so important is that there is no USP that differentiates your business from others.

Price

All customers want the same thing-the best deal. But, price is not the real issue. Most people do not buy on price alone. They consider price, but there are usually more powerful reasons they buy.

For example, 7-Eleven stores are 40% more expensive than a typical grocery store. Why can they get away with this? They carry many of the same products, but people are willing to pay extra for their USP - convenience, fast in and out. LensCrafters glasses are 30% to 70% more for their USP - speed of delivery. They built an entire giant company on delivery of glasses in one hour, instead of two or three days as used to be the norm. Rolex watches cost $1,500-$5,000 without precious stones. You can buy a watch which keeps perfect time for $10. Why would you pay more? You pay more for their USP - prestige and quality.

Customers will come to you because your USP promises to solve their problem. So you want a USP because it defines your market, and it enables you to focus your marketing on the customer that is most likely to buy.

If you have a roofing business you may want to define your market with a good USP that focus on just residential jobs. You may not have the capacity, equipment, financial capital or man power to do large commercial jobs, so you don't want to waste you marketing efforts and money trying to get large commercial jobs. Do what you can deliver best. Tailor your package and USP to their specific needs.

You can create a great USP by focusing on what you're good at, or want to be good at, and deliver that to your prospective customers. USP can be speed, convenience, location, delivery, quality, variety, taste, colors, fun, snob appeal, exclusivity, rarity, financing, expertise, design, reliability, extra services, specialization, price, guarantees, excitement and dozens of others which may be unique to your industry.

Give prospects a definite reason to call you with a great USP.

Once you solve the market's problem with your USP, you can now focus on the **delivery** of that USP in a dazzling manner. When you deliver on your USP promise well, customers will not only return to you again and again, but also refer you again and again.

 *Write down your USP in less than two lines.*_____
_____

Example: "Absolutely, positively, overnight" or "The Utimate Drive Machine"

Brand

Your USP and your personal brand are intertwined. Everyone and every company has a brand, or reputation. It can be good or bad. Your personal brand is established by your behavior, appearance, skills, communications, honesty, trustworthiness, your online presence, and how you handle problems.. It is how you are viewed, how you describe yourself, and how others perceive you. In business it is how you service and treat your clients and customers.

If you say Rolex, an establish brand comes to mind. You will know about its prices, quality, guarantee, prestige, and that it will be consistent worldwide. You know what you're going to get because of the brand. That positive brand is one of the reasons people will go to you rather than another brand.

Apple
Coca-Cola
Toyota
IBM
Rolex
BMW

Your personal brand is similar. When people you know say your name, what images and characteristics come to mind? Are you courteous, clean, dependable, trustworthy, loyal, etc.?

Your personal appearance counts. It reflects on your personal brand. People don't want to refer a person who looks dirty, disorganized, slovenly, etc. If you checked into a hotel and found your room with dirty mirrors, dirty toilets or bugs, how would you brand that hotel or the hotel chain?

Your personal brand is affected in the same way by a slovenly appearance, sloppy sales material, etc. Your brand or reputation is priceless-if negative, it's difficult to dispel, if positive it's a great asset for getting business through referrals.

Figure out what you want to be known for, and who your audience is. Package that into a brand reputation and then deliver on it.

√ *How can you brand yourself?*_____
_____
_____
_____

Example:
A logo, or unique tag line

Part 3

Referral Sources

The sources of immediate referrals are everywhere. They are nearly endless. Of course, you are thinking about getting referrals, but just as importantly, think about giving them. A great referral network is a two way street. The more you give the more you get.

3.1 Customers

Think of all your customers, current and past There may be hundreds or thousands. These are all the people who liked and trusted you enough to purchase your product or service. They already know you. Hopefully, you have kept in touch with them and offered them good service after the original sale. If not, it's time to start. These are people and companies that can become an immediate source for new leads and referrals. These are the people who already know about the benefits that you have brought them.

√ *List 5 five customers you will ask for referrals, recommendations, etc.*

1. _____
2. _____
3. _____
4. _____
5. _____

3.2 Friends, neighbors, relatives and casual acquaintances

These are people who want you to succeed. They know you already and hopefully you have cultivated a good reputation with them. They each know dozens of other people who may have an interest in your product or service. Let them know that you're expanding your business and you would be grateful for any new clients and customers.

√ *List three friends, etc, you will ask.*

1. _____
2. _____
3. _____

3.3 Vendors and suppliers

Business associates want you to succeed. After all you may be selling some of their products. Vendors want your goodwill and are usually willing to enter into a mutually beneficial relationship. Also, their employees might be candidates for what you have to offer.

√ *List three vendors you will ask for referrals and recommendations.*

1. _____
2. _____
3. _____

3.4 Employees

Cultivate good relationships with employees, especially in large companies where they may be buried away in accounting or the shipping department. Let them know you want referrals and leads for new business. Encourage them to recommend you by various incentives like bonuses, cash, praise, additional attention or gift certificates. Make up company business cards with their names. The act of getting non salespeople involved in bringing in business binds the employee to the fortunes of the company. Employees make human contact with all sorts of people who may need your company's products or services, but don't know how to sell them.

√   *If you have employees, what three things can you do to encourage endorsements, recommendations, etc.*

    1. _____

    2. _____

    3. _____

    4. *Example: cash "finder's fee", time off, etc.*

3.5 Competitors and related businesses

There are all sorts of ways that competitors may be able to help each other. They may not have the capacity or resources to fill a prospective customer's needs. They may be at the high-end of the market and you might be at the low-end of the market, or in different physical locations. You could easily set up exchange of leads, or some other kind of finder's fee. There may be people in your business, but have different specialties. For example, dentists are always referring people to oral surgeons. Real estate, insurance and mortgage agents can be a great source for cross referrals. General contractors and specialty contractors can easily help one another. The list is almost endless for associated or related businesses. But, you must cultivate the competition.

√ *List who you will contact in a related or competitive business.*

1. _____
2. _____
3. _____

√ *What deal will you propose? What is the mutual benefits?*_____
_____
_____
_____
_____

3.6 Current and unconverted prospects

These people are in a unique position. You have already made a presentation of your product or service, and they are aware of the features and benefits. There are all sorts of reasons that prospects have not become clients, but it does not prevent them from referring others to you. .

Uncle Fred may be their current supplier and your prospect is stuck with that relationship, but it doesn't prevent him from referring you. Never leave a current or unconverted prospect without asking who they know that might have an interest in what you do.

√ *List three who you will contact.*_____

1. _____
2._____
3._____

3.7 Formalized lead networks

Organizations to exchange business leads are a consistent source of referrals. Most of these groups meet weekly with the express purpose of generating business for their members. Most of the groups are local, but some, like Le Tip, International, Business Network International (BNI) and Main Street Chamber have thousands of members and hundreds of chapters. Many of these groups only allow one person per profession to join a chapter so it limits competition within the group.

Every member knows the purpose of the group and attends for the same reason - to generate leads and referrals. Ideally those leads will come with some degree of warmth and introduction.

These groups serve three purposes, (1) to develop a mutually beneficial exchange relationship with all its members, (2) to teach each of the members how they can prospect for each other, and (3) to get access to the hundreds of persons strong spheres of influence of each member.

You might want to create your own group. Find four to six others whom you trust and would benefit from a referral organization. Explain the concept to each and begin having meetings. Build the group one at a time. Be sure to be generous with your leads to other members.

√ *Look up a local group and call about their next meeting. List here.___*

_____

_____

3.8 Fellow members of church, social and recreational groups

Members of hobby groups, little leagues, athletics, churches, fraternal groups that have similar interests as you. They usually know what you do and can easily become sources of business.

√ *List three.*_____
_____
_____

3.9 College or school

School friends are great source of referrals. They know you and are easy to talk to about mutually developing your business through referrals. You usually have more than one thing in common which make developing referral networks easier.

√ *List three school colleagues. How can you help each other?*_____

_____

_____

_____

_____

3.10 Retired Executives

This is a good one to get introductions to hard to reach and isolated executives. Executives are typically very difficult to contact with the usual marketing methods, like telemarketing, direct mail, etc. Many times these are big ticket sales. An introduction by a retired colleague can very valuable.

√ *Do you know any? List them.*_____

_____

*What kind of incentive will you propose for their contacts?*_____

_____

_____

_____

3.11 Internet Network

In a survey done in April 2012 the Nielson group says the online reviews are the second most trusted source of information with a huge 70% of the consumers saying they trusted the reviews. Only direct word of mouth recommendations carry more weight.

LinkedIn is a good source of like minded business people. Get Dan Sherman's excellent book, Maximum Success with Linkedin, for details on how to use this important business site. He points out how influential Linkedin is and dozens of ways to use it.

Dan Sherman sets out a step-by-step method how to use LinkedIn as your own free mini website to create thousands of potential contacts, build your personal or company brand, and sell your products and services. See the LinkedIn Profiles of Sherman, Vivek Von Rosen, and Greig Wells, all LinkedIn experts to see excellent examples of how to use LinkedIn.com to get business and introduction to millions of potential customers.

Get on Linkedin.com, create a profile and get involved. Turn your LinkedIn Profile into a benefit filled commercial for yourself. Every time one of your primary links puts you in contact with people they know, make a self introduction to that third person using the primary person's name and reference. Tell them what you do and ask for information about them. Ask if you can help with any of their concerns. Add them to your Linkedin contacts and email list if relevant and prioritize them for periodic contact.

If any of your good contacts are not tech savvy, help them set up a Linkedin account and profile. Add them to your contacts and Recommend them on your account. Point out to them how beneficial it would be to them.

You can use LinkedIn Recommendatoins and Endorsements in your other marketing materials.

LinkedIn is a huge worldwide network where you can establish yourself as an authority in your field quickly. You can also customize it for local use.

√   *Go to Linkedin.com and Facebook.com and open an account. Set up your Profile and become active. Begin adding contacts. Date you opened account._____*
—

Date you get to the first 100 contacts._____

Date you get to 500 contacts_____

3.12 Associations and Organization Networking

Get involved in associations that might be relevant to your offerings. Attend Chamber of Commerce, Lion's Club, Rotary and other organizations mixers and events. I know of insurance agents who are active members of attorney's bar associations because a major part of their business referrals come from attorneys. My local locksmith is a member of the local apartment association.

√ *List two groups you would like to join.*_____
1._____
2._____

3.13 Centers of Influence

Centers of influence include, CPAs, attorneys, industry and business leaders in your community. A good way to meet them is through volunteer work for civic and charitable causes in your community. Another way to meet them is through introductions from people you already know.

Most businesses already have an accountant and lawyer. Ask who they are and use your customer's name as an introduction.

√   ***Who do you want to meet? What is the mutual benefit?*_____**
_____
_____

3.14 TV, Radio, Newspapers, Magazines

Introduce yourself to the writers, editors and talk show hosts of these media sources. Offer to become a "go to" expert on your specialty. When events happen in your communities that are related to your field, they can call you for explanation and/or comments. For example, in our city we have a weekly medical segment on the local network TV affiliate that features local doctors. We have a local weekly business radio show that brings various business specialists to talk about their area of expertise. Our daily local radio talk show interviews businesses in the community.

You can even talk to the media station about sponsoring or buying your own show. In most small markets they are very receptive to new programming offers.

√   *List who you want to contact and how you want to contact them. Find out about them through the internet and watch or listen to their media. Contact the station.*

_____

_____

_____

3.15 Networking

Because this is such an important potential source of referrals, let's spend some time talking about how to use this source.

Networking is based on meeting people face to face, but it also includes the concept of Six Degrees of Separation, first introduced by Krigyes Karinthy in 1929, and later popularized in the 1960 play by John Guare. It is a theory that everyone is just six steps away, by way of introduction, from any other person on the planet. In 2002, the theory is said to be proven by studies at Microsoft and Colombia University to be about 6.6 steps.

Whether it is 5, 6 or 7 steps is immaterial. What is true is that it does not take that many steps to meet anyone in business, especially if they are in the same industry. Remember, everyone you meet knows 200 plus other people.

We have described four different networks above which have slightly different characteristics, but good networking follows a few simple principles that make them all potentially valuable.

The more commonality the network has with your personal and business interest, the more valuable they tend to be. Since you have more in common it tends to be easier to communicate and understand the interests of the members.

Networks can have as few as one, or thousands of members. Networking within general groups, like Chamber of Commerce mixers is generally not as productive as those where you already have commonality among members. The point here is that you want to focus your time and efforts where you are most likely to get a higher return on your investment of money and time.

For the best success, keep in mind the definition of networking: networking is meeting people and cultivating *mutually* beneficial, give and take, win-win relationships that support each other.

With the definition in mind let's look at some of the characteristics of good networking.

1. Networking is a 50/50 proposition. It's all about give and take. Your goal should be to always try to give more than you receive. This principle will result in feelings of likability, credibility and openness. Try to show more interest in *their* business and goals. They will tend to show more reciprocity by following this policy.

2. Good networking looks at areas of mutual benefit where the connection can reward all the people involved.

3. Networks support all its members. You want to look to share the resources and knowledge. Network partners are connected by deeds not phony interests. Try to introduce and connect members to each other when ever you feel there may be a mutual benefit. Send articles, books, and information when it would be valuable to other members. Have the attitude "I saw this article and I immediately thought of you." Your thinking of them is a powerful motivator to get them to think of you.

Warming questions

When you meet people for the first time, it is handy to have a few questions to help start and sustain a conversation. Note that they are all oriented towards the person you meet. Here are a few questions from Bob Burg's wonderful book, <u>Endless Referrals</u>. They all support networking principles:

71

1. *How did you get started in the_____ business?* Let them tell their story while you listen. They will tell you all sorts of information that will allow you to carry on the conversation.
2. *How long have you been in the_____ business?*
3. *What are the coming trends in your business? What direction do you think it will take?*
4. *What are the biggest changes that have taken place since you've been in the business?*
5. *What do you think are the best ways to promote your business?*
6. *What separates you and your company from the competition?*
7. *What advice would you give to someone just starting out?*
8. *What one word would you like people to use in describing the way you do business?*

All these questions are designed to elicit good, positive feelings. Let them brag on their successes. Let them demonstrate their knowledge, and tell you if there might be a mutual beneficial relationship.

 Learn the warming questions.

Networking Dos and Don't

> **Do**
> 1. Adopt a great attitude. You should be open to networking at all times and places. Smile, it invites comment and introductions. Be friendly, relax and enjoy meeting people. The great referral master, Dr. Ivan Misner, suggests you act like a host. You will be more outgoing, introduce people to each other, and will be in a more giving mode.
> 2. Work the crowd. It is why you are at the event. Take the initiative. Meet as many people as you can. Meet *new* people. People you already know are comfortable, but that's not why you are there.

Renew acquaintances and contacts, but don't hang out with them, unless that is specifically why you are there.

3. Introduce yourself to the host and express your thanks.
4. Decide who you want to meet and seek out centers of influence, like organization officers, guest speakers, organizers.
5. Start conversations with the above warming questions.
6. Collect appropriate business cards and make notes on them.
7. Follow up quickly where appropriate.

Don't
1 Sell. It is very annoying and not what you are there for.
2 Complain about the facilities or accommodations.
3 Have too much to drink.
4 Monopolize a person's time.
5 Be stand-offish.
6 Put people on a mail list without their permission.

Encourage network members to refer.

Now that you have a good idea *who* can refer, let's look at all the things you can do to set up conditions for them to want to refer you and stimulate them to give you recommendations.

Needless to say you can't just walk up to friends, neighbors, business acquaintances, etc. and say give me the names of all the people who you know that might be interested in what I have the to sell. Getting referrals is based upon the depth and kind of relationships you have with people. What you ask and how you ask is also based upon that relationship.

Surprisingly, you can get referrals, introductions, and recommendations from a tremendously wide range of relationships. It could be from a thin rapport with the shopkeeper that you have just met by asking for information on the shop next door; or asking a close and longtime relationship for referrals by giving a full-blown presentation on how they can help you.

√ *Condition your contacts that you want and expect referrals. Start laying the foundation for getting referrals by taking these actions.*

- Get the mindset that you have something valuable to offer. You must believe you're doing a real service that people want and need.
- Be sure that your product or service is indeed a good one. If not create one that is.
- Create a unique selling proposition that give reasons for people to purchase from you above all others in your industry. Demonstrated your USP continually.
- Show a genuine interest in people. Ask questions about their business, products, and interests. Ask how you can further their interests.
- Inform people why your products and services are the best value and offer the most benefits.
- Remind people of the benefits that your relationship has brought them.
- Assure people that you will be professional and that you will not disturb any existing relationships they have with those whom they referred to you.
- Let them know that most of your business comes from satisfied customers who refer.
- Ask your contacts to call the referral to let them know you will be contacting them and to put in a good word on your behalf.
- Keep in contact with people who give you referrals. Send them cards, tweets, letters, e-mail, articles of interest, hobby information, and referrals. Do personal and family favors where you can.
- Ask for referrals when they have expressed satisfaction or just bought your products or services. If they have not purchased from you yet, ask them for people who they believe may have an interest in your products and services.
- Be sure to inform your sources of the results of the referrals that they have given you. Thank the source whether the referral was fruitful or not.

74

- Ask for advice on expanding or managing your business.
- Never forget to send hand written thank you notes for any favors, purchases, or consideration shown to you. Send a gift when appropriate. Gratitude has a way of attracting similar feeling and actions.
- Above all, **deliver** what you say you will.

Here are some special networking rules for longer term sale cycles and professionals:

1. Don't be impatient. Take the long term view. Developing a good recurring business network takes some time. Make the commitment to keep at it.

2. Select centers of influence that are already involved with your target market. If you are interested in developers, try to network with CPAs, attorneys, etc. who already have developer clients.

3. Contribute to the network members by soliciting clients on their behalf. Recommend them, pass out their cards, work for their charitable causes. Send them any articles from newspapers and industry publications that might be of interest to them. Volunteer for their association's committees and boards. Recruit new members for the organizations. Get involved with charitable causes of those centers of influence. This will bring you contacts and introduction to many who it may be difficult to meet in a business setting.

4. Spend more time with the centers of influence than with your peers and colleagues. Entertain them in settings where you can build trust and have uninterrupted conversation. Golfing, hunting, fishing, ball games, lunches are all great ways get extended time.

5. Go after several centers of influence at once. Don't limit yourself to just one CPA, attorney, business leader, etc. You will find many times they often know each other.

6. Send business and referrals to the network members. Be sure to let them know a referral may be coming their way. Make a direct introduction between the two if you have a chance. Let the Law of Reciprocity take effect.

 What two networking events will you attend in the next 30 days?

_____

_____

Part 4

A System

All the people you meet by networking, referrals, and sales calls will go into either your manual, or computerized customer management or internet funnel system. Your system gives you a place to record all the customer's and referral's information, and any interactions you have with them.

4.1 A System

The point of a system is to keep in touch and stimulate interest in your product or service. Most people need numerous contacts with you before they will purchase. A study from Darnell Corporation shows that 80% of sales are made after the fifth sales call.

- 40% quit after the first contact.
- 72% stop after the second contact
- 84% give up on prospects after the third contact.
- 90% gave up after the fourth contact.

Since only 10% of salespeople made more than four calls, it means 10% are getting 80% of the business.

Referral marketing is built not only on persistence, but also on building trust and credibility through the follow-up process. Like a personal relationship, you're not going to be very successful by proposing on the very first date. The series of contacts is meant to build that trust and credibility. You build a relationship over time and develop an understanding of the client's needs and wants.

One of the big advantages of referral marketing is a great deal of the relationship development has been previously satisfied by the recommendation of the trusted referral source. The source has indirectly vetted you in the referral's mind.

Although persistence is extremely important, keep in mind the 80/20 Rule. 80% or more of your referrals will come from 20% of your sources. Focus on this 20% -cater to them and pamper them. If you make them special, you will become their favorite vendor. Set up a calendar of scheduled contacts that allocates your time and budget to the most productive sources and prospects.

Your contacts will consist of two different kinds. The first kind is one to one personalized contacts. They are your highest priority, because you have established a personal contact.

The second kind has a broader reach of people on your list. These people usually have some degree of interest and have arrived on your list by opting in to some sort of offer you have made to them. It might have been a newsletter, information request, promotional announcement, or personal contact. Because they don't know you as well, you need to start building trust and credibility. Gradually, these list people will begin to self identify their level of interest by their response to your contacts. Prioritize and pursue them according to their level of interest. Do not send information to the people on this list unless you have permission to do so. If your list is not overly large, follow-up by phone call to new list members. It can have a very powerful effect in creating an initial bond with them.

Now you need to decide whether you want to use a manual, or a computerized customer management system (CRM).

If you use a spreadsheet you can create a star ranking categories and add them as you go. You can get more formal and use customer management software (CRM), like Salesforce, ACT, or Goldmine. These software programs have the information forms set up to begin gathering information on people you already know and those you will meet.

You can also use LinkedIn as a contact system. As a bonus it is free.

Manual system
Create a list either on 3x5 cards or spreadsheet of everyone you know from the above sources. You don't want to waste your time, so, prioritize them with a 5 star system.

If you use 3x5 cards, score their perceive value as customers or sources with one to five stars in the upper right corner. After you have your initial stack of cards, put the twenty contacts with stars on top and begin working them first. As you meet new people, score them and add the appropriate star ranking.

Create a calendar for scheduling follow ups and contacts. You can use Outlook or similar calendars. Many times these contacts are made for "good will" so that customers don't feel the only time they hear from you is when you are trying to sell something.

If you use a manual system, begin gathering information. Create a form with the following information and copy it. The form should have the following: (See a copy of the form in the Resources section)

1. **Name**, including any nicknames, titles, and what they prefer to be called.
2. **Company,** position and what responsibilities they have. How long have they been there? Did they work their way up or do they come from another company? What do they specifically do, because titles can sometimes be misleading?
3. **Address** and contact information. This would include information from the business card and the myriad ways to contact people nowadays, but also personal contact information if possible. The personal information may come over time as you get to know them better. Where someone lives may give you strong clues as to income levels and lifestyle choices.
4. **Referred** by information. This should include the date you first make contact and circumstances under which the referring source gave you the referral. For example, maybe the referral asked the source for someone to prepare their taxes. Or the referral may have asked the source who fixed their dishwasher, etc.
5. **Age and place of birth**. Sometimes it is easy to obtain and is a natural part of the getting to know process. For example, in insurance, tax preparation, accounting, counseling businesses, their date of birth will be a natural question.

6. **Marital status**. How long and the spouse's name.
7. **Family.** How many children do they have, what are their names, ages, and what kind of activities they enjoy. The information here can be of tremendous value in creating a closer bond with the referral.
8. **Nationality or ethnic group**. Tread lightly here and don't make too many assumptions. Is this an important topic for them? Is there any commonality with family, friends, sports, clubs, etc.
9. **Educational background**. Degrees, licenses, credentials? Where did they go to school? What levels did they achieve? What kind specialty training do they have? Are they involved in any ongoing trainings or certifications?
10. **Religion**. If there's an immediate commonality it will tell you about some of their views, holidays, lifestyle restrictions, etc.
11. **Political views**. This area can be dangerous to pursue, but also can be a strong bond. Note any political comments here.
12. **Automobile.** What type do they drive and why?
13. **Hobbies and recreational choices**. Whether someone likes to race motorcycles or play chess can give you strong clues as to the kind of gifts and articles, that might be appreciated
14. **Associations** and groups.
15. **Public awards or achievements**.
16. **Reading materials** and television time. What kind of magazines and books and television do they enjoy?
17. **Investments**. Are they risk takers or conservative? Are they invested in real estate, stocks, bonds, or other businesses?
18. **Health issues**.
19. **Drinking habits**. You would not want to be giving a bottle of wine to teetotalers or an alcoholic.
20. **Leisure and vacation** times. Are they active or passive? Do they like skiing or cruises? Do they like the mountains or the beach?
21. **Buying habits.** Are they impressed with prestige labels or are they thriftier? What kind of clothes, jewelry, watches and accessories do you see around them?

22. **Best friends or mentors**. Any common friends?
23. **Miscellaneous**. General notes of insight on anything that is not covered above.

The LinkedIn system provides much of the above information provide by the prospective customer themselves.

Obviously, all of the above information gives you great insight into the person you are dealing with. It can help you find areas of commonality, personal interests, and emotionally sensitive points. The information can help you select the right gifts, cards, articles of interest, areas of conversation, and areas of mutual exchange.

Now you have the start of a management system for contact and follow up. Regardless of the system you use, you should set aside time to "work" your system daily. "Working" the system is comprised of all your follow-ups, meetings notes, mail or contacts. **Make contact time into a daily ritual.** If you are new in a business you will have more time to prospect and follow up.

 Choose a contact system and begin gathering information on potential referral sources and customers.

4.2 How to Follow Up.

After the referral or recommendation, follow-up quickly. Don't let it cool. There are usually three ways to make initial contact with the referral. Ask your source for guidance as to which one you should use. The initial contact with the referral should be used to:

- Judge whether the prospect may be a fruitful referral.
- Get to know each other better.
- Try to assess the prospects needs and wants.
- Set up future contacts.

Find out as much you can about the referral, primarily from your source, but also from the internet, Facebook, Linkedin, Twitter, and other available sources. Find out if the source has spoken to the referral about you, and what information he's passed on. This information will let you tailor your initial contact to make the best first impression.

Face-to-face meetings are the most valuable because both you and the prospect can assessed one another. Don't go into a full-blown sale mode unless that's what the prospect expects or they have expressed an urgent need for your product or service.

A second means of initial contact might be in a written form, a letter, e-mail or card. The written format lets you carefully structure how you want to introduce yourself. Start with the name of your referral source and what your relationship is with him. And if you have previously met, remind him of the occasion or the event. Suggest a meeting at a mutually convenient time and date. Offer to send any relevant information. Finally, let the referral source know the results of this correspondence.

If the source recommends, you could follow-up with a telephone call. Again, start by mentioning the referral source and your reason for calling. Send any information they require. If the source mentioned a specific problem the referral has, you might gently bring it up. Nevertheless, go softly before you know the referral better, or they want to know specifically what you have to offer. Suggest a meeting to get to know each other.

Once you have a better assessment of the referral, you can tailor your future contacts appropriately. The above scenario is geared toward building a longer-term type of business client. Depending on the product, you may have a shorter term sales cycle and need to be more aggressive in future follow-ups.

You may want to a send small useful gift like a notepad with your picture and contact information on it. You might leave specialty imprinted items, like a pen or letter opener.

If you have authored an "expert" book, leave a copy. An expert book with your name and picture on the cover is tremendously impressive and immediately establishes you as a "go to person" in your business. Let the book do the bragging for you. Our company helps business people write and publish "expert" books that establishes your expert status (Xpert Publisher,775 827-1775, or BDSConsult@gmail.com.

Of course, send referrals a personalized thank you note regarding the meeting, their interest, or a purchase.

With their permission, you might put the referral into a periodic contact system to consistently update and inform the prospect about your products or services. You might use short messaging service (SMS), tweets, e-mails, newsletter, postcards, both personal and voice mail, personalized FedEx or priority mailings. What ever follow up you use, be sure not to annoy a referred prospect. Don't let the communication become all about you. Try to offer value and address their needs with each contact. Keep the referral source appraised of the results.

√ *Specifically, what system will you use?*_____

_____

_____

_____

Part 5

29 Basic Strategies with 100 Twists

There are really only 29 or so basic referral methods, but there are hundreds of twists based on those methods. The twists you can adapt to your particular industry or category of business, practice or profession. Listed below are the primary strategies followed by examples of particular types of businesses that can use the strategy.

5.1 Competitor's exchange

Exchange referrals and leads with companies and people in the <u>same</u> business, but <u>different geographic</u> areas. You may agree to exchange the leads or pay a "finder's fee" or commission. It is rare someone will refer you just because of a monetary reward. They do it because they believe in you and your performance.

- This concept applies to almost any locally oriented business. This may also apply to businesses where state licenses are required and the local business or practice is not licensed in a neighboring state. Another reason is that the service might be too expensive or unwieldy to be provided to a distant locality. Several industries have set up formal nationwide referrals, likes Allied or Mayflower household movers, florists like Teleflora, and Bloom Net. This may apply to businesses like attorneys, CPAs, tax preparation, aircraft and boat services, contractors, musical bands, trucking and transportation services. Many of these relationships can be set up through industry associations, organizations and meetings.
- A great way to meet distant competitor is through LinkedIn.com.

√ *List which two competitors will you contact immediately?*

_____

_____

√ *List three other competitors you have contacted by way of associations or LinkedIn.*

_____

_____

_____

5.2 Pay a fee or give away a product or service for an X number of referrals

- For example a hotel could offer a free stay in a luxurious room for every eight or 10 people that you send them. Hotels could use this to get travel agents or company travel arrangers to repeatedly use their facility.
- Direct TV is using a similar program where if you sent them a referral, they would give you a free month of cable service. All you have to do is get an account number of the referring party to DirecTV when they sign up for their service. The referring source gets a month worth of TV service valued at anywhere from $50 to $200, and Direct TV would get a minimum of a year's membership worth from $500 to $1000.
- This concept works well for apartment complexes. Tenants refer prospective tenants to the apartment and the tenant receives a rebate or discount on the rent. Every apartment complex should remind their tenants of this benefit every month. It will save a lot of advertising money.
- This strategy works particularly well in service industries where unused capacity is used as a give away to create new customers.

√ *What proposal will you make? To Whom?*_____
_____
_____
_____
_____
_____

5.3 Timing is everything

The concept of timing is particularly important for generating referrals. Whether you are active, rather than passive, makes a huge difference as to your rate of referrals.

- You want to ask customers for referrals when they are happy with your product and service. When you are finished with an interview or have closed a sale, always ask, *"By the way, who else do think might need my services?"* They have just made a decision to trust you, so what better time to ask for referrals. They're much more willing to suggest someone they know who would make a similar "wise" purchase. They want friends, acquaintances, business associates to validate their purchase seeking the same benefits.
- Ask for referrals when a customer, client, patient has expressed satisfaction. For example, if a dental patient says something like, "These new veneers sure look great", the dentist would ask if anyone else in the family would like the same great smile.
- Businesses should keep either business referral cards, survey or business reply cards for the customer to fill out at the moment of satisfaction. Once you have the okay from the customer, you use these reply cards to call the referrals, invoke the customer's name, and tell them how happy the customer is with this product or service.

√   *Write down the date you asked for a referral after a compliment. This will help you to remember to ask.*_____

89

5.4 Thank you gifts where they get people to talk about you

- I know car dealers that send thank you notes with balloons and a personalized coffee mug to the office or workplace of the new purchaser. All the coworkers are asking what it's all about. Be sure to include several business cards with the delivery.
- Congratulations on the birth of the a new child, an anniversary, a birthday, a promotion, an awarding of a big contract, or any other significant events in your customer's life can be celebrated with balloons, a trophy, or flowers to the workplace or office.
- Set up reminder on your calender.

√ *Who?*_____

What occasions?

_____

_____

5.5 Create a gift certificate

The idea here is to create a gift certificate or special discount coupon that customers can give away to *their* customers, friends, and acquaintances, etc. This kind of gift certificate creates three winners. It allows your current customers to give up something of value that makes you look good to *his* customers. The person who receives the certificate gets a discount or something free when he redeems it at your business. And finally, you win because you are very likely to get a new customer and create good will for your current customer.

- We created an entire marketing program for restaurants that use post card sized gift certificates to attract many new customers. As the diners are winding up their meal the wait staff asks about their food and dining experience. The waiter then asks if they would like to give away a free entrée, meal or drink to their friends. If the answer is yes, the waiter leaves a pen and one or more certificates at the table for the customer to write in the name(s) of the recipient. When the customer is ready to pay the bill and leave, the waiter picks up the certificate(s). If the certificate has an address on it, the restaurant mails them out, if not, they let the customer take them to give personally to the recipient. The post card certificate can vary slightly depending on the wishes of the restaurant owner, but it says something similar to this:

"I just had a wonderful meal at (name of the restaurant). I thought you might like to try it too. Here's a gift certificate for a free (entrée or other or dollar amount) from me and (name of the restaurant). Enjoy."

(name of giver)   (Restaurant owner's signature)   *expire date*

- Here is an example of an Ophthalmologist using a similar strategy with his patients:

Dear Mrs. Martin, (his client)

Since I began recommending LASIK corrective surgery to my patients, I have discovered that LASIK patients are the most enthusiastic patients I have. If you love your Lasik results as much as my other patients do, I'm sure you are already recommending it to your family and friends.

In order for you to share the advantages of LASIK, I have enclosed a certificate for free LASIK exam that you can pass on to others. If they decide to become LASIK patients I will also give them a $300 discount off the regular fee. Simply fill in your name and theirs and have them call my office for an appointment.

And to thank you, I will give you a free annual eye exam and your choice of any designer frames we carry in our office.

Thank you in advance for sharing your enthusiasm for LASIK and your confidence in me with the people important to you. You can be assured that I will provide them with the same quality service that you have come to expect from me.

Sincerely,

Dr. Paul Miller.

- My plumber regularly mails me a "Thank You" post card with the following on it:

"Thank you for choosing Sierra Plumbing Heating and Air for your recent service. Approximately 80% of our business is from repeat and referral customers. We value our customers, and to say thank you for choosing us, we're including two valuable coupons below. The first coupon is for your next service. The second coupon is for you to give to a friend or family member who has not yet tried Sierra Plumbing Heating and Air."

Attached are the discount two coupons for $10 off.

- John Jantsch, in his book, <u>Referral Flood</u>, tells a great story about a shoe shine guy that gives out four of his business cards to customers, and tells them he will "refund" 25% of his shine fee on his next visit for every one that is presented back to him from a new customer. This can be done with any service.

- Obviously, you can create a similar type postcard/letter certificate for almost any kind of business. This is particularly good in new services businesses where you have excess time available and there is little out-of-pocket product cost. The real leverage of this approach is that you have your customers working for you.

√ ***Write down your gift certificate offer. To Whom?***_____

_____

_____

_____

_____

_____

_____

_____

5.5   Exchange with related industries

Every business has other businesses that are complementary or related to it that are natural connections. Because they are complementary to each other you can easily exchange leads, referrals, recommendations, introductions and even fees and commissions. The "exchange rate" is whatever you agree on. I prefer to build a relationship and skip the monetary exchange. Just try to give more than you get.

- A perfect example of this relationship is between wedding photographers and caterers, wedding planners, disc jockeys, limousine services, venue locations, jewelers, travel agents, and wedding dress shops. A smart owner in any of these businesses will set up relationships with the other. They can pass out business cards, brochures, verbal recommendations, and even discounts or gift certificates for each other's businesses. If I were new in any of the above businesses, I would form alliances with each of the wedding related businesses. The average couple spent over $29,000 on their wedding in 2012.
- I have a pharmacist client who makes a personal visit to neighborhood doctors', and retirement homes to introduce himself. He then sends out occasional pizzas and his business card to their office staffs. He says he gets tremendous amounts of business from these sources as a result of the goodwill created.

Other possible combinations of related businesses:
- Dentists and oral surgeons, orthodontist.
- Real estate agents and mortgage brokers, appraisers, home inspectors, escrow companies, alarms, specialty contractors, handyman, carpet cleaners. etc.
- Decorators and home furnishing stores, window treatment and flooring stores.
- Pool cleaners and pool contractors.

- Hair salons and cosmetic surgery (hair implants).
- Carpet cleaners and flooring contractors.
- Auto sales and auto accessories.
- Different kinds of specialty attorneys.
- Bookkeepers and tax preparer's, CPAs, Enroller agents and tax negotiators.
- General contractors and dozens of kinds of specialty contractors.
- Travel agents and hotels/motels, rental cars, tour operators.
- General practice and specialty doctors, physical therapists.
- Automobile repair and tires, and accessories.
- Lawn services and landscape contractors, real estate agents, nurseries.
- Locksmiths and apartments, real estate agents and hotel/motels
- Plumbers and electricians with apartment owners and managers.
- Kennels and pet groomers and veterinarians, pet stores.
- Sign companies and real estate leasing agents, and all retail businesses.
- Hot tubs and pool supplies.
- Movers and apartments, real estate agents.
- Credit card processors and CPAs, bookkeepers.
- Tailors and dry cleaners, clothing stores.

Use your imagination. There are hundreds of possible related natural connections that can be mutually beneficial.

√ *Name three you will contact._____   _____*
_____ What arrangement will you make?_____
_____
_____
_____
_____
_____
_____

5.7   Unsolicited praise

This strategy cost very little and it has a magic effect on those people that you recommend. They instantly become a silent sales force for you. Send out a letter or e-mail to your vendors, suppliers and even customers and clients praising those that help you.

- Here's an example of a real estate agents' letter: (names and emails have been changes for the book)

Letterhead or email

Dear Judy, (real estate client)

"As a way of saying thank you to the people who help me successfully complete our closings, I'm sharing their names, web addresses and phone numbers. If you need the kind of help they provide, please hire them.

They demonstrate the highest level of professionalism, and follow through on what they say they will do. I can't guarantee their work, but I recommend them highly. I'm not financially compensated by them, but just want to spread the news of their fine work.

Bill Jones, of Success Mortgage Company,(bill@SuccessMortagage.com, 213-555-9990) is a thoroughly professional mortgage broker. He has saved several deals with his creative and attentive services for my buyers. If it's possible he will find a way.

Judy Smith, at Best escrow, Judy@Bestescrow.com, 213-555-8880) is the best. She creates and provides our real estate documents in a timely manner and communicates superbly with both buyers and sellers."

..........etc, etc.

Susan Martin, Local Realty

The letter goes on to praise an inspector, appraiser, handyman, and a couple of other people. After each receives the note, do you think each would be appreciative for the praise and might send any home sales referrals her way? Do you think they would be even more helpful in the future? I think so. Could you adapt a similar note to your list of customers, vendors, etc.?

- You could take this concept one step farther by creating a personal "Angie's List" that you send out to your network periodically. It would include an endorsement and praise for those people whom you use to get things done. You would list their names, contact information, a brief description of what they do, and how they have helped your business. You should categorize them much like a yellow pages directory. Of course, you would only include the network members with their permission.
- You can also use this strategy on <u>LinkedIn.com</u> Recommendations. Not only are the Recommendations appreciated, but many times they will reciprocate the Recommendation thereby boosting your expert status on LinkedIn. See Dan Sherman's book, <u>Maximum Success with Linkedin</u>, on details of how to get and manage your Recommendations.
- Now turn around and use these Recommendations in your other marketing materials.

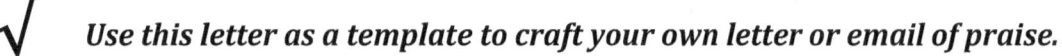 *Use this letter as a template to craft your own letter or email of praise.*

5.8 Associations, organization, clubs.

Become active in associations and organizations that are filled with members who could use your products and services. The important thing here is to become an <u>active</u> member of the group. It creates goodwill and demonstrates you have a real interest in furthering the association's goals. Almost every business listed above has organizations that could use your services.

- For example, if you are a locksmith or contractor you might want to become active in apartment associations or hotel/motel associations. The point here is that you meet a lot of people who are natural customers with the services and products you offer.

- Volunteer for boards, committees, or serve as an officer of the group. Your status jumps immediately and the spot light makes you a more valuable person to know. It usually brings you into more intimate contact with more people quickly.

√ *Name two organizations you will join.*_____

_____

5.9   Discount for bringing a friend or group

Offer a discount for bringing a friend or group works great for any kind of seminar, training, or event. The incremental cost of bringing in extra people to an event is minimal, so you can afford to discount *each* member of the group. For example, an event might normally cost $200. per person, but if you bring two people you might discount $20 for each. In a company training setting you might have the company bring 10 people and only charge $125 for each. This is another way to have the attendees become your enthusiastic salespeople. This is a subtle endorsement and referral from the original person to the additional people that attend.

√   *Create an offer.*_____

_____

_____

_____

_____

5.10 Vendors

This is an excellent and easy source to ask for referrals. They already know you and are usually eager to have you expand your business, as it usually indirectly helps their business.

- If you are a tax preparer, financial planner, stock broker, small bank, or any other service that is used regularly by employees, talk to any of your vendors about a system to introduce you to their employees. You might give a seminar, or have them distribute literature, put inserts into paycheck envelopes, or numerous other ways that reach a larger number of people at one time.

√ *Which vendors?*_____
_____
_____
*What can you offer?*_____
_____
_____
_____

5.11 Joint ventures

Create a joint venture where you have your good source sell your products/services. You could split the net income or you could pay all the mailing expenses. The act of helping you is an implied endorsement or referral. Make these ventures a two way street. Support any of the source's activities.

- This may be accomplished though consignment at retail locations.
- Any of your referral sources that have large mailing lists could tout your goods with their mailings or allow you to insert product information in mailings.
- It is very common for internet marketers to sponsor and recommend products to each other's mailing list.

√ *Who?_____ What offer?_____*

_____

_____

_____

5.12 Bird-dog.

Pay a commission or incentive to anyone you know to keep their eyes and ears open. This is not necessarily a warm and fuzzy referral, but a bird-dog will certainly sing your praises for money. This group of people becomes an informal sales force for you.

- Offered to give some kind of incentive for referrals. These incentives could be a commission based upon the gross sale, or net profit or some other formula. There are hundreds of ways you could express your appreciation for business directed your way. You can give unexpected movie tickets, lotto tickets, dinners, subscriptions to magazines of their interest, gift certificates, gift cards, books, CDs of their favorite music, flowers, etc. If you're in a profession where it would be unethical to pay a commission, you might donate to their favorite cause, or to promote their business somehow.

- This method is used by automobile salespeople quite widely. There's no reason this method cannot be used for any number of products and services. I know a plastic surgeon that gives huge discounts to patients who refer other patients.

- An investment sales firm approaches retired executives and former government regulators with a proposal that they will pay 10% of the business they can refer from these big decision makers.

- This contact method is useful for big ticket life insurance and estate planning policy sales. If the industry ethics prohibits paying finder fees, other legal ways can be found to incentivize the retired executives.

√ *Name three or more people to "bird dog" for you.*_____

    1._____

    2._____

    3._____

5.13 Internal company referrals

If you are already doing business with a company that has other departments or branches, you could ask for referrals from those you are working with to refer you to the other departments. Since you have already demonstrated your value within one branch it is highly likely they would be willing to refer you to another area of the company.

- I know a sandwich shop that started catering by preparing lunch sandwiches for a nearby company that had over 200 employees. He asked the department head if he could put in a good word for him with the other departments, and has subsequently built over 30% of his business in just this one company in just a few months.
- Do you sell products where departments or branches have their own budget? This is certainly a place where you should be asking for a referral.

5.14 Marketing Material Referrals

Be sure to put some kind of referrals or testimonials in your marketing material. You can ask for referrals on pre-paid cards or surveys. If you could say something like, *"If you know anybody who would enjoy this (product or service) like you do, just fill in their names and addresses and we will be glad to send them a catalog."*

- Almost any direct mail catalog or subscription service could use this very inexpensive device.

- Authors and other merchandise sellers should ask for reviews on all electronic merchandising outlets. Reviews are a form of testimonials that reduce the fear of customer's buying. If you have 100 reviews of your book or product on Amazon.com, it certainly lends credibility to your publication or product.

√   *What phase will you add to your marketing material?*_____

_____

_____

_____

5.15 Postioning

Position yourself as "my business grows mainly by referrals, because we do such a great job, I expect the clients to refer others to our office". Here are two examples:

- A dentist (or other professional) would be well served if he would tell a patient the conditions of becoming a longtime patient. He would say something like,

  "I want to thank you for coming to see us. We want to provide you with the best possible services, so we ask a few considerations from you. We ask that when you make an appointment that you keep it, or give us plenty of notice to fill your appointment time. That way we don't have to charge you for a canceled appointment time. We ask that you pay after services are rendered, so we don't have to increase the costs for billing and bookkeeping. Another way we keep our costs to you down is to avoid a lot of advertising and promotional cost, so we ask that you refer us to your friends, family and acquaintances. I'm sure you would not mind referring us if we are doing a super job for you. Is that right?"

  This sort of initial meeting or interview about the ground rules of the doctor/patient relationship is tremendously helpful. It also lays the groundwork for asking for referrals in the future.
- My dentist has a "Welcome to Our Practice" brochure he gives each new patient. It describes his procedures and lists all his services. The brochure discusses appointments, scheduling and financial options.
- I built a script for a home decorator that emphasizes that she only works with a new client by referral from existing clients. The initial interview is conducted as a favor to the existing client. The purpose of the meeting is to interview one another; to see if their personalities mesh well; and to be sure she will have fun doing the project. She emphasizes she's doing the job

not because of the fees, but she loves creating new home and office environments. She implies that if the conditions are not met, she will not take the job. The great thing about these conditions is, she means it. She has refused to take jobs because she concludes from the interview the client would not be a joy to work with.

Wouldn't it be great to spend your time working with ideal clients who are the kind people you want to work with. In this case, after the job is finished she usually follows up with an unexpected gift, like a subscription to Architectural Digest, Home and Garden, a vase of flowers, or an additional accessory.

Good positioning solves lots of problems:
- Payments are made more promptly.
- Communication and cooperation is better.
- You feel more invigorated with higher energy.
- You get rid of clients who bore, frustrate and drain your energy.
- It makes getting and asking for referrals much easier.

√   *How can you create a stronger position?*_____
_____
_____
_____
_____

5.16 Guest programs

Invite current members to bring guests at a big discount or for free, then offer guests a membership, or gather contact information for e-mails and postcards and other forms of follow-up. Have the guest register when they come in. Thank the member for bringing the guest if they are with him at the time, or if not, send the member a thank-you card.

- Any sort of membership organization like health clubs, shooting ranges, martial arts studios, dance studios, etc. can use this strategy. With proper follow-up it is not unusual to have 30% to 40% of the guests become members.

√ *If this fits your business, create a guest program, registration and follow   up   membership   offer.*

_____

_____

_____

_____

_____

_____

5.17 Continuous Follow up

When customers and clients hear from you regularly, they are more inclined to give you referrals and repeat business. You demonstrate, by follow-up, that they are not lost and forgotten. Set up a continuous follow-up system for customers and prospects. There are several systems that can automate this important technique. Keep on top of their thinking by using newsletters, e-mails, cards, voicemails, videos and twitters. Mike Koenig has a great system called Instant Customer at www.TrafficGeyser.com. Once set up, the system allows you to follow-up in six different ways *automatically* for any length of time. The system even allows you to scan business cards you get at meetings and network functions for a follow-up within hours of your meeting. It is very impressive to be able to follow up so quickly and in so many ways. Your conversion rate will increase dramatically. This stands in contrast to most people who gather cards at a meeting, show or event, and never follow-up, or only get to a few over a period of time.

It is important to send articles and other notes of interest that are not sales oriented. Try to avoid the impression that the only reason you're contacting them is to sell something.

Always offer a certificate or incentive for them to give to friends for a free trial of your product or service. Offer something of value like a report relevant to their business.

√ *Create a follow up system. What method? Date to start?*_____

_____

_____

5.18 Borrow credibility

You can further enhance your credibility and status by appearing with famous people or those that are well known to your prospective audience or market. Volunteering to participate in fundraising or promoting good causes can bring you into their sphere of influence. Displaying a picture of getting out of a helicopter with Donald Trump would help anyone with real estate interest in New York. Being on a speaking stage with Fortune 500 executives helps your business credentials and opens up avenues of contact and conversation.

- Advertisements on television borrow credibility from celebrities and famous athletes all the time. They lend their names and pictures to products in hope that their fame will boost product credibility.
- ExpertPublisher.com has an excellent program to secure the use of the logos of ABC, NBC, CBS, FOX and others on your marketing materials, web sites, LinkedIn and other social media sites. The logos show your contributions to their publications and programs. Because the logos are so well known they lend tremendous creditability and authority to your products and services. "As seen on:"

√ *Contact ExpertPublisher.com to explore displaying media logos in your marketing materials and your contributions to the mass media.*

5.19 Surprise Discounts

Find a way to give a price discount or gift to the customer that generates new referrals. Figure out how much it cost you to generate your average sale in advertising and marketing costs. Use that amount as your incentive. How can you adapt this to your business?

Surprise

- Here's the way one air conditioning and furnace company uses a surprise discount. In this case, because the sales ticket is relatively high you can afford a relatively high discount or gift at the end of the presentation and after the sale is closed, the salesperson offers the customer several business cards and expresses thanks. He says,

   "Your business has been referred to us by (name) and we would like to give you $50 off the good pricing you have already negotiated. If you would like to do this with one of your friends, we will be paying you $50 for the referral and also give the same $50 to your friend." The salesman then asks for the name and contact information for that friend. The beauty of this particular method is that you're not actually giving away anything until you have a sale.

- Here is a creative way to use a surprise discount or refund a mortgage broker uses to get a steady stream of referrals. The broker sends the customer a surprise refund. After each deal is closed the broker sends a personal note surrounded by two crisp five dollar bills and a bunch of loose change. The note reads:

   "Hi Susan,

111

I've enclosed $10.79 in this envelope. It took a little less time to work on your refinancing that I had budgeted. Thanks for making it so easy"
        Sam

Also clipped to the note are two business cards. When was the last time you got an unsolicited refund from any person you do business with? Probably never. I'll bet that the average recipient of this special envelope will retell the story dozens of times. It's certainly worth the $10.79 investment.

This works well because it's totally unexpected and an expression of gratitude. How can you work a surprise refund into your business?

√   **What surprise can you create?**_____

_____

_____

_____

_____

5.20 Show off your work

This works well with anything you create. For example:

- The previously mentioned interior decorator always asks the client during the job, if the client will hold an open house for friends, neighbors, etc. when the project is completed. They serve refreshments  and give a tour of the newly finished home. The decorator is at the event, passing out business cards and snoozing with the guests. She always gets at least one new assignment from the opening.
- This strategy also works for any builder or contractor. Host a grand opening; invite anyone who had a hand in the project, possible buyers, etc. Meet the guests, collect cards, and follow up with a "thanks" for attending card. These events usually open up a new world of contacts.
- Film, documentary makers and commercial artists can display either at dedicated showings or as part of related events of the clients. A local bank might allows one of their customer-artist to display art work in the lobby.

√ *Does this apply to you? Set an event and time to "show off your work".*_____

5.21 Survey

Send follow up quality control questionnaires or surveys to current and prior clients asking for their feedback. Usually, these are forms with check off boxes and an area for comments. Make it easy for them. Always pay for the return postage with a pre addressed or business reply envelope or card. At the bottom of the card should be a space  and lines for them to write in names, telephone number and address for referrals. These forms also serve the purpose of reinforcing your perceived desire to improve the service to the client.

- You might use the comments as part of your testimonial display and include them on your marketing materials.

5.22 Testimonial Letters and Reviews

Testimonial letters and positive reviews are important social proof of your ability to deliver. Take any opportunity to ask for them and use them anywhere you can. They are another form of recommendation and referral. They really work. They go a long way in reducing the fear of commitment from the customer and show what sort of results this new customer can expect.

- In my early selling career I worked for a sign company where the principal selling tool was a book of hundreds of pictures and testimonial letters of previous sign installations. The reason these testimonial letters were so important is that we made a cold call right off the street where we were a total unknown quantity to the business owner. On top of that, in most cases, we were an out-of-state company. The sale amount was anywhere from $500-$5,000 in a single cold call presentation. So it was imperative that we had ample proof and credibility before they would give us a deposit check. We made extensive use of these testimonial letters and pictures and made offers for the prospect business to call the testimonial givers.

If you use testimonials in your business, be sure they are displayed well in a neat and clean manner. Don't just tack up a letter from a satisfied customer on the bulletin board near the sales counter. Have them framed or organized into a nice presentation.

You should use testimonials and third-party endorsements in your sales and promotional materials if you get the okay from the source. Sometimes you may only use a pull quote from a letter along with identifying the source.

- One of the great benefits of the Internet is it gives you the opportunity to use both sight, sound and the written word to exhibit your testimonials. It is easy to use a hand-held smart phone to create short videos of your customers singing your praise? These, of course, can be played back on smart phones and electronic tablets when talking with prospective new customers. You can easily add them to your website, your LinkedIn profile and Facebook accounts.

- Make it easy for clients, patients and customers to give you testimonials. Bill Cates, in his book Unlimited Referrals, suggest a terrific follow up system to get testimonials. He says, after you ask for a testimonial endorsement and the source agrees, follow-up shortly with a note thanking them in advance for the letter they will be sending. This becomes a subtle reminder that they agreed to provide the endorsement. If you have not received the endorsement after a respectable period of time, you can call the person on the phone and say *"that's okay I know you're really busy. Would it be helpful if I put a few of the thoughts that we discussed on paper for you? You can edit it or rewrite it anyway you like and send it to me on your letterhead, OK?"* They always agree.

- Every waiting room or reception area should have a binder of testimonial letters and comments displayed prominently that reinforces your abilities and satisfaction of clients.

√ ***Organize and display testimonials. Date started._____***

5.23 Group presentation requests

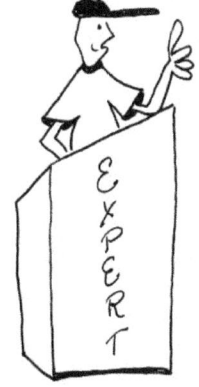

Any time you are able to get in front of a group of people find a way to ask for referrals. This can be done in a number of different ways. Always offer the host several ways for the guests to contact you.

- If you are a band or caterer at a wedding ask the host if you can display a small discrete card at each one of the guest's tables. Make an announcement near the end of the wedding of your band's name and contact information. Or you can ask the host to do this.

- I have had several magicians, clowns, entertainers and speakers at our events and home parties, and I always get the comment,"That guy was great. Where can I get a hold of him?" Be sure the host has your card or contact information, and be sure to send a thank you card to the host.

- Seminar trainers and professional speakers should always close or follow up with some sort of questionnaire or survey about the presentation. The important part of the survey is that not only does it let you know how well you did, but you should have a check box where the attendees can ask for more information. Always leave some way for the attendees to contact you. There are many ways for attendees to "opt in" to your contact network. Seminar trainers are good at this prospect gathering method, but entertainers seldom have a method to contact the group members.

 Create something so that attendees can contact you._____

5.24 References

You have done all the right things to get 95% to the close, but at the last moment, the prospect hits you with a final challenge. He needs two references that have had satisfactory results from your product/service. Hopefully you have prepared ahead of time with a few references that the prospect can call. Make it a major goal to set up references in each market you serve.

Ask several of your satisfied customers if you can use them as references, that is, someone a new prospect can call to get an "unbiased" opinion of your product or service. This becomes a form of a testimonial that also lets the customer know you are seeking referrals. Even if the prospect does not know the referral, it is a powerful third party enforcement to help you close the sale.

When you complete a job always ask if you can use the customer as a ref erence. Encourage new prospects to contact current references. They seldom do, but it becomes a great risk reducing strategy to put the new prospect at ease. In some cases, you might want to prepare a list of reference clients and leave it with new prospects.

Assure your references that his duties will not be time-consuming or frequent. These are usually the two reasons most references will balk at serving. Be sure to reward your references for their help, but not to the extent that they feel "bought". The best reward you can give them is to send them new business.

√ *Contact three customers or clients to ask for if you can use them as references.*_____
_____
_____

√ *Create a list of satisfied customers and references you can leave with prospects.*

5.25 Direct Request

Don't be shy about directly asking your current clients for help. A direct request of your clients and others asking for referrals certainly lets them know that you are actively trying to expand your business. Below is a letter which one of my accountant clients sends to clients before the end of each year. He usually gets 2 to 4 new clients from this letter every year. Note how he has tried to jog their memory and gives a place to write a record of them. Adapt it to your business.

- *"Dear Client and Friend,*

  I want to take this opportunity to thank you. I've been preparing your taxes and providing you with other accounting services for some time. I consider you a very valuable client and also a friend. I very much appreciate the trust and confidence you have placed with me concerning your private financial matters.

  Since this is a time of the year that brings tax preparation to a higher visibility, many more people are talking about it. By your continued patronage, I assume you're satisfied with the services I have provided in the past. Being a successful person brings you in contact with other successful people: associates, employees, customers, friends, acquaintances, and relatives.

  May I ask you a favor?

  Like most businesses, I'm always looking to expand. A referral from you would carry a lot of weight. If you feel comfortable providing referrals, I would appreciate any. If the subject of taxes, business planning, business problem solving, or consulting comes up in conversation, please suggest they give me a call. If you would prefer I would be glad to call and introduce myself on your recommendation.

  Just to jog your memory, I've listed a few people who might be in need of my services:

Name	Phone number

People filing taxes the first time_____
New business associates_____
Vendors and suppliers_____
People thinking about going into business_____
New customers_____
Your doctor, lawyer, cobbler, etc._____

Please call if you have any introductions. As always, I'll try to send business your way.

Thanks for your help, and I hope the New Year brings you happiness and prosperity.

Signed_____

P.S. Of course, all of your's and your referral's financial matters remain strictly confidential.

- *My dentist asks for referrals in his waiting room via a large framed sign next to the exit door. He calls it his "Share the Care" with patient's family and friends.*

√ **Write a letter or e mail and send it to current customers.**
Date started_____

5.26 Cross promotion

Set up cross promotional activities between you and several of your network members. You see this done all the time between new motion picture openings and fast food restaurants on a nationwide basis. You can do the same thing locally. Set up relationships with complementary businesses. If you are a photographer, you could go to wedding dress shops, caterers, disc jockeys, party planners and limousine services and set up a cross referral network.

- If you are a wedding photographer, you could create a folder of brochures or promotional materials from a caterer, limo service, disc jockey, wedding planners, etc. The kits could then be given away by each service to promote all the other services. This way you would gain access to customers and prospects that you would never see just promoting your own service.

- If you are an automobile repair business you could arrange cross promotions with a tire shop or automobile accessory shop. You could give special discounts or special services for each other's customers. Each one of you could have promotional material of the other's in their shops. The possibilities are limitless.

- Macy's and other department stores send out their promotional catalogs with several other flyers, such as perfumes, cosmetics, watches, etc. that are piggy backed in the packages. The flyer companies get to split the costs and gain access to Macy's giant mailing list.
- Many of these promotions are ideally built around holidays such as New Years, Valentine's Day, Easter, Memorial Day, Independence Day, Labor Day, Halloween, Thanksgiving, Christmas, Store Anniversaries, President's Day, St. Patrick's Day, etc.

√ *Name two clients with whom you can cross promote*_____
_____
_____

5.27 Asked to be introduced

An introduction is a mild form of referral. It does not have the same fear element attached to it because an introduction merely suggests an invitation to explore the other person. It is much softer. The introduction does not have the risk of judgment or obligation to follow up with action. An introduction has no expectation of quality of service or performance, but because there is a mutual connection between parties, there is an implication that a similar relationship may have similar favorable results.

An introduction suggests the parties run in the same circles, have similar status, and similar interests. You are clearly not a stranger. For example, if Donald Trump introduces you as a real estate agent to another party, it is not as strong as a referral or recommendation, but still carries with it a suggestion of mutual respect and acknowledgment of the competence of the agent. After all, people seldom introduce a dud. Introductions are easier to get and give, but still carry a positive influence.

Introductions need to be followed up in a gentler fashion. They need to be more subtle with a suggestion of mutual benefits. If you can give something of value, like a referral, it will almost certainly open a more in depth conversation. For example, a telephone follow-up conversation might go something like this:

- *"Hello. Mr. Jones, this is Bill Smith calling, we were introduced by Jim Jones a few nights ago at the Children's Charity Ball. How are you? I thought it was a wonderful event to raise lots of money for the children's Society. Since you are in the Real estate loan business I thought you might want to talk with a contractor friend of mine who is planning a new shopping center project."*
- (Explore his interest in the possible referral. If he would like to go further, set up an appropriate convenient meeting. Now the door is open to develop a larger relationship.)

Introductions can lead to unusual, but lucrative opportunities. One of the best I know of is a story told by Michael Lewis, the author of the number one national bestseller, <u>Liar's Poker</u>. He retells an account of being invited to a black-tie, fund-raising event at the British Royal Palace by a distant cousin. He goes to the event and is fortuitously seated between the wives of two managing directors of the famous investment house Salomon Brothers. After many questions as to his career choices from one lady, he asked, and she promised she would introduce Mr. Lewis to her husband, the managing director. True to her word, she made the introduction. After an interview he was offered a job at the prestigious firm, by-passing the unpleasant vetting of Salomon Brothers recruiters and landing ahead of 6,000 applicants. This chance meeting and introduction enabled him to secure a lucrative and prestigious job at the investment house.

- Introductions can be easy to generate and lead to interesting places, especially if you have a destination in mind.

√ *List three people you want to whom you want an introduction._____*

_____

_____

Who will introduce you?_____

_____

5.28 Bartering

Setup or join a bartering group. Bartering is a natural way to create more word-of-mouth buzz. Joining bartering groups exposes you to dozens or hundreds of other businesses. If you can barter something rather than write a check it helps greatly with your cash flow. You can get rid of excess inventory in a much more cash efficient way. You could sell the inventory at a discount or liquidated it for much less than it's worth or get full value by converting it into bartered goods and services.

- Professionals with excess time are ideal prospects for bartering.
- Radio stations are famous for trading your services and products for advertising time.

√ *Look up a bartering group on the Internet in your area. Investigate and join if appropriate. Name_____Telephone*

_____

5.29 Endorsements

If you doubt the power of endorsement or recommendations look at advertising done everday by famous athletes and celebrities. They prove so valuable that the celebrity endorsers are paid millions of dollars to have their names attached to products. Tiger Woods, Michael Jordan, and others are considered so powerful that they not only advertise products related to their sport, but also products entirely unrelated.

- *One of the nation's largest collection agencies uses endorsements to drive their entire marketing effort. The company gains the endorsement of over 400 hundred major industry associations and organizations and uses that written endorsement to sell the association members and others in the industry on their services. The collection agency goes to medical associations, dental associations, contractor associations, insurance associations, retail associations etc. Each Association usually has hundreds, if not thousands of members. The Association gets a fee for every collection the collection agency makes for its members.*

    - *As an example, the Southern California Medical Association (doctor's) recommends the collection agency services via its letterhead. The collection agency sales staff uses the letter to get appointments and close the sales on the strength of the collection agencies record and the association's recommendation. These associations' endorsements have a powerful effect on the decision of the prospect. It reduces the doctor's fear of making a decision and makes appointment setting a breeze.*

    - *Many radio stations produce and air 30 second commercials from its advertisers endorsing the station's effectiveness and their satisfaction with the advertising results. The radio stations sales staff uses these recordings in their presentation to prospect new business advertisers. Each of the endorsers has agreed to be a personal reference to help close the sale. So both the radio station and its advertisers gain a benefit because the radio station gains endorsement and the advertising client gets free advertising during that endorsement.*

- *With the endorser's permission you could use it in your marketing materials, radio, TV or print media. If you can think of a way you will both benefit, it may not cost you anything.*
- *LinkedIn provides a perfect place to gather Endorsemenst and Recommendations.*

 What local organizations, associations or celebrities could you get to endorse your product or services. How can both of you gain from an endorsement? List two_____

Part 6

Resources

- Books
- Referral Information Form
- Gift Ideas
- Lead Clubs
- Book Writing Guide
- Follow up System

Books

Burg, Bob, *Endless Referrals*, McGraw-Hill, New York, 1996

Cates, Bill, *Unlimited Referrals*, Thunder Hill Press, Silver Springs, Maryland, 1996

Cialdini, Robert, *Influence*, Collins Business, 2007

Crandall, Rick, *Marketing Your Services*, McGraw-Hill, 1996

Edwards, Paul and Sarah, Douglas, Laura, *Gettting Business to Come to You.*, Perigee Books, New York, 1991

Gee, Jeff and Val, *Super Service*, McGraw-Hill, New York, 1999.

Jantsch, John, *The Referral Engine,* Portfolio Trade, 2012

Kennedy, Dan, *Ultimate Marketing Plan*, Adams Media, 2000

LeBoeuf, Michael, *How to Win Customers and Keep Them for Life*, Berkley Books, 1987.

Michaels, Nancy, and Karpowicz, *Off the Wall Marketing Ideas*, Adams Media, Avon, Massachusetts, 2000.

Misner, Ivan, and Robert Davis, *Business By Referral,* Bard Press, Austin, Texas, 1998

Phillips, Michael and Rasberry, Salli, *Marketing Without Advertising*, Nolo Press, 1986

Pinskey, Raleigh, *101 Ways to Promote Yourself,* Avon Books, 1997

Port, Michael, *Book YourSelf Solid.* John Wiley & Sons, Hoboken, New Jersey, 2013

Sherman, Dan, Maximun *Success with LinkedIn*, McGraw Hill, New York, 2013

Stanley, Thomas, *Networking with the Affluent and Their Advisors*, Irwin Professional Publishing, Burr Ridge, Illinois, 1993

Stanley, Thomas, *Selling to the Affluent*, Irwin Professional Publishing, Burr Ridge, Illinois 1991

Von Rosen, Viveka, *LinkedIn Marketing: An Hour a Day*, John Wiley & Sons, 2012

Willeford, Dean, *Cash Out,* Expert Publisher, Reno, Nevada 2012

Willeford, Dean, *The iCorporation,* Expert Publisher, Reno, Nevada, 201

Information Form

1. **Name**, including any nicknames, titles, and what they prefer to be called.

    _____

2. **Company,** position and what responsibilities they have. How long have they been there? Did they work their way up or did they come from another company? What do they specifically do, because titles can sometimes be misleading?

    _____
    _____

3. **Address** and contact information. This would include information from the business card and the myriad ways to contact people nowadays, but also personal contact information if possible. The personal information may come over time as you get to know them better. Where someone lives may give you strong clues as to income levels and lifestyle choices._____
    _____

    _____
    _____

4. **Referred** by information. This should include the date you first make contact and circumstances under which the referring source gave you the referral. For example, maybe the referral asked the source for someone to prepare their taxes. Or the referral may have asked the source who fixed their dishwasher, etc.

    _____

5. **Age and place of birth**. Sometimes it is easy to obtain and is a natural part of the getting to know process. For example, in insurance, tax preparation, accounting, counseling businesses, their date of birth will be a natural question.

    _____

6. **Marital status**. How long and the spouse's name._____

7. **Family.** How many children do they have, what are their names, ages, and what kind of activities they enjoy. The information here can be of

tremendous value in creating a closer bond with the referral._____

_____

8. **Nationality or ethnic group**. Tread lightly here and don't make too many assumptions. Is this an important topic for them? Is there any commonality with family, friends, sports, clubs, etc._____

_____

9. **Educational background**. Degrees, licenses, credentials? Where did they go to school? What levels did they achieve? What kind specialty training do they have? Are they involved in any ongoing trainings or certifications?_____

_____

_____

10. **Religion**. If there's an immediate commonality it will tell you about some of their views, holidays, lifestyle restrictions, etc._____

_____

11. **Political views**. This area can be dangerous to pursue. Make a footnote of any political comments here. This could be an area of strong bonding._____

_____

12. **Automobile.** What type do they drive in why?_____

_____

13. **Hobbies and recreational choices**. Whether someone likes to race motorcycles or play chess team can give you strong clues as to the kind of gifts and articles that might be appreciated._____

_____

14. **Associations** and groups._____

_____

15. **Public awards or achievements.**_____

_____

16. **Reading materials** and television time. What kind of magazines and books and television do they enjoy?_____

_____

17. **Investments**. Are they risk takers or conservative? Are they invested in real estate, stocks, bonds, or other busineses_____

_____

18. **Health issues**._____

19. **Drinking habits**. You would not want to be giving a bottle of wine to teetotalers._____
___

20. **Leisure and vacation** times. Are they active or passive? Do they like skiing or cruises? Do they like the mountains or the beach?_____

_____

21. **Buying habits.** Are they impressed with prestige labels or are they more thrifty? What kind of clothes, jewelry, watches and accessories do you see around them._____

_____

22. **Best friends or mentors**. Any common friends?_____

_____

23. **Miscellaneous**. General notes of insight on anything that is not covered above._____

_____

_____

Gift ideas and incentives

1. Gift cards
2. Lotto tickets
3. Movie tickets
4. Subscriptions, magazine, journals, newspapers, newsletters.
5. Gift certificates
6. Books
7. Picture note pads, printed post it notes.
8. Specialty imprinted items, cups, hats, magnets, pins, bags, shirts, calculators, calenders, etc.
9. Auto accessories
10. Donations to charities or causes
11. CDs of favorite music
12. Dinner or lunch for not only source, but for their staffs.
13. Sports tickets, especially for local events
14. Customized fortune cookies
15. Christmas, anniversary, birthday gifts
16. Flowers, balloons, candy, plants, cakes.
17. Trophies, plaques.
18. Any gift or favor for referral source's children.
19. Door mats
20. Customized postage stamps
21. Free lessons- golf, tennis, etc.
22. Customized returns address labels.
23. Soft wear that improves their business.

Formalized Lead Clubs

Main Street Chamber.org   on the Web

Business Network International   1-800-688-9394

Le Tip, International -find a chapter   on the Web. Letip.com

Expert Book Writing Guide

XpertPublisher   ConsultwithPro@yahoo.com
Mass media logos   ConsultwithPro@yahoo.com

Follow up and contact system

Traffic Geyser   TrafficGeyer.com